Ancient Rome

1 0 0 0 FACTS

First published in 2008 by Miles Kelly Publishing Ltd
Bardfield Centre, Great Bardfield, Essex, CM7 4SL

Copyright © 2007 Miles Kelly Publishing Ltd

This material is also available in hardback

2 4 6 8 10 9 7 5 3 1

Editorial Director Belinda Gallagher
Art Director Jo Brewer
Editorial Assistant Carly Blake
Page Layout Rick Caylor, Ian Paulyn
Picture Research Manager Liberty Newton
Picture Researcher Laura Faulder
Production Manager Elizabeth Brunwin
Indexer Hilary Bird
Reprographics Anthony Cambray, Stephan Davis, Ian Paulyn

British Library Cataloguing-in-Publication Data
A catalogue record for this book is available from the British Library

ISBN 978-1-84236-958-6

Printed in China

www.mileskelly.net
info@mileskelly.net

www.factsforprojects.com

Ancient Rome

1000 FACTS

Rupert Matthews

Miles Kelly

PUBLISHING

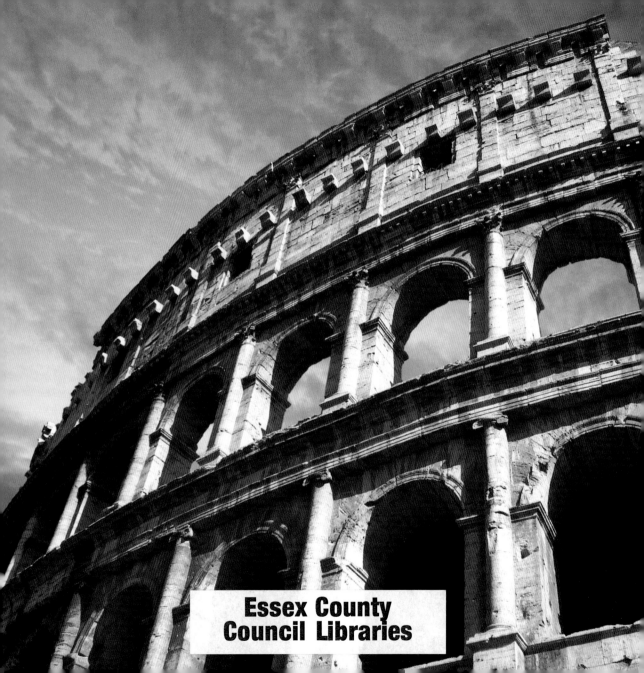

Contents

Contents

TECHNOLOGY AND THE ARTS

GODS AND FESTIVALS

Prehistoric Italy

- **Italy has been inhabited** by humans for around half a million years. Modern humans arrived there about 70,000 years ago. They roamed the land, hunting animals and gathering plants.

- **About 8000 years ago**, the first farmers began living in Italy. These people planted crops and kept animals. Farming was introduced to Italy by migrants arriving by sea from the Middle East.

- **Italy is the peninsula** that extends into the Mediterranean Sea, south of the Alps. Islands such as Elba, Sicily and Sardinia are also part of Italy.

- **The Apennines Mountains** run down the centre of Italy, from north to south. Chains of smaller mountains and hills extend over much of the rest of the country.

- **The largest area** of level land is the great plain that lies south of the Alps. This is the Lombardy Plain. The valley of the river Po runs through the plain.

- **By about 800 BC**, the area north of the Po Valley was inhabited by tribes belonging to the Celtic peoples. These tribes belonged to a culture that extended west to Spain, north to Britain and east to the river Danube.

▲ *Prehistoric Italy was occupied by several different peoples. There were also Greek colonies near the coasts.*

- **At this time**, the lands south of the Po Valley were inhabited by a number of different tribes and peoples. These peoples included the Samnites, Etruscans and Latins. They spoke varieties of a language called Italic – although the Etruscans had their own language.

- **In the 200 years** that followed, many Greek colonies were founded around the coast of southern Italy. The Greeks brought with them new ideas, gods and ways of living. One the most important ideas was that of the city state.

▲ *This gold bowl, made in about 600 BC, comes from a Greek colony on Sicily, although the style shows influences from Phoenicia in the eastern Mediterranean.*

- **A city state** is an independent state that consists of one large city, surrounded by farming lands and some smaller towns and villages. The Italic peoples began reorganizing their states as city states, but not all of them followed Greek ways of government.

- **The Etruscans founded** a number of city states that were allied to each other. These cities became rich and powerful. The Etruscans soon dominated the economy and politics of a large part of Italy.

Romulus and Remus

- **The early history of Rome** is shrouded in myths and legends. Early Romans did not know how to read or write, so they passed down their history as oral tales and poems. Over the years these stories became rather mixed.

- **Later Romans** studied the old tales and legends, many of which were written, or strongly influenced, by the Greeks. They used these to put together an account of the first 300 years or so of the history of Rome. This helped to reflect Rome's growing importance.

- **According to legend**, Rome was founded by two brothers named Romulus and Remus in 753 BC. By that date, the brothers had already led exciting lives.

- **Romulus and Remus** were the grandsons and heirs of King Numitor of Alba Longa, an Etruscan city. When Numitor's brother, Amulius, grabbed the throne by force, he threw the baby brothers into the river Tiber to drown.

- **However**, the two boys were washed up on a sandbank where they were found by a she-wolf, which fed them on her milk. Eventually, the boys were found by a shepherd named Faustulus, who brought them up with the help of his wife, Larentia.

- **When they grew up**, the brothers lead the local shepherds. They founded their own state on the hill where they had been cared for by the wolf. This hill was the Palatine, by the river Tiber in the land of the Latins.

- **Romulus had the job** of building a wall around the hilltop. Remus said the wall was too low to keep out enemy soldiers. To prove this, Remus jumped over the wall in a single bound. Romulus was furious and killed his brother.

- **In this way**, Romulus became king of Rome. He then kidnapped all the unmarried women from the region of Sabina to be wives to his shepherds.

▲ *A famous legend tells how Rome was founded by Romulus and Remus, twin boys who had been suckled by a wolf.*

FASCINATING FACT

One day in 716 BC, Romulus was reviewing the Roman army when a thunderstorm appeared and the king was struck dead by lightning. He was buried beneath a black marble slab at the foot of the Palatine.

● **The Sabine men** marched to destroy Rome, but the Sabine women refused to let their fathers kill their husbands. A treaty was drawn up between Sabina and Rome.

11

The Roman kings

- **All of the early kings** are surrounded by myths. Historians think these may contain some clues as to what actually happened. According to myth, when Romulus died, he left no children so his role as king was taken by Numa Pompilius, a Sabine man.

- **As king**, Numa helped to establish a calendar that was unique to Rome. Certain days were set aside for religious activities, other days for government elections and festivals. Numa ruled Rome until 673 BC.

- **The third king** was Tullus Hostilius, who reigned for 32 years. He led Rome against Alba Longa, a city of Latium, which was conquered. Tullus was murdered by Ancus Martius, grandson of Numa Pompilius, who became the fourth king.

- **Ancus Martius** either conquered or formed alliances with other states in Latium. He built the port of Ostia at the mouth of the river Tiber and extended Rome to include the Aventine Hill and the valley between that hill and the Palatine.

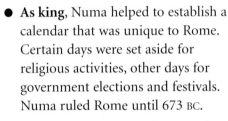

◀ *King Numa, the second king of Rome. His reign was peaceful, and he helped to establish religious rites and ceremonies.*

- **When Ancus died** in 616 BC, his children were young, so an Etruscan named Tarquin the Elder was made guardian. Tarquin took the throne for himself, using his money to build new temples and public buildings.

- **Tarquin the Elder** was murdered in 578 BC by the sons of Ancus. The throne was then taken by Servius Tullius, who was married to Tarquin's daughter.

- **Servius Tullius reigned** until 534 BC. During that time he expanded Rome to include the Esquiline, Quirinal and Virminal hills, by which time the state had 84,000 inhabitants.

- **Servius was murdered** by his daughter Tullia and her husband Tarquin the Proud, grandson of Tarquin the Elder. Tarquin the Proud then became the seventh king of Rome.

- **Tarquin the Proud** built beautiful new temples on the Capitoline Hill dedicated to the Capitoline triad of deities – the three most important Roman gods. However he ignored the wishes of the people and tried to control the Senate (Roman council) by threats and bribery.

FASCINATING FACT
Another story says that In 510 BC, Sextus, son of Tarquin, attacked the noblewoman, Lucretia. Lucretia's husband, Collatinus, and his friend Brutus Lucius Junius, expelled Tarquin and his family from Rome. There were no more kings of Rome.

The early republic

- **After the expulsion** of Tarquin the Proud, a a new form of republican government began to evolve in Rome. It was based on the idea that power should be in the hands of the people.

- **Tarquin the Proud** fled to his Etruscan relatives. He asked King Lars Porsenna of Clusium to lead an army to Rome to return him to the throne.

- **The invasion was halted** at the Sublician Bridge by the guard Horatius Cocles. He held the bridge alone until the Romans cut it down, then he swam back to Rome.

- **The various cities** of Latium formed the Latin League in 338 BC. The League fought a long series of wars against the Etruscans. These ended with the capture of the Etruscan city of Veii in 396 BC.

▶ A bronze statue of an Etruscan warrior from about 400 BC. He carries a small round shield and has elaborate body armour made up of small plates of metal.

- **In 451** BC, the Romans appointed a board of ten wise men, the *Decemviri*, to review and reform the laws of Rome. This was in response to years of unrest by the citizens and the growing size of the city. The reformed laws were engraved on 12 tables of brass and set up where everyone could see them.

- **In 390** BC, an army of Celts swept down the Po Valley, led by their king, Brennus. At the Battle of Allia, the army of the Latin League was defeated.

- **The Celts** captured Rome. Most people had fled, but a few held out on the Capitoline Hill to guard the temples. A sneak Celtic attack was defeated when the sacred geese in the Temple of Juno raised the alarm.

- **The Romans agreed** to pay the Celts to return to the Po Valley. When they complained that the scales used to weigh the gold tribute were unfairly weighted Brennus replied, "*Vae Victis,*" meaning 'Woe to the conquered'.

- **In 340** BC, the Latin War began. Some Latin states tried to fight the power of Rome, others sided with Rome. After two years of fighting, the Latin League was replaced by Roman rule.

FASCINATING FACT
The Samnites were defeated at the Battle of Sentinum in 295 BC after a long war. Many Greek cities in southern Italy, and other states, also came under Roman rule after this.

War with Carthage

- **By 265 BC**, Rome was the most powerful state in Italy. Other cities or states south of the Po Valley had either been conquered by Rome or were allied to Rome.

- **That year**, Italian mercenaries captured the city of Messana on the island of Sicily from Hieron, king of the independent city state of Syracuse. They asked Rome for help, while King Hieron asked for aid from his ally, Carthage

- **Carthage** was the most powerful city state in the western Mediterranean. It stood in North Africa, near what is now Tunis. The wars between Rome and Carthage are called the Punic Wars because the people from the area around Carthage were known as Punics.

- **The First Punic War** ended in 241 BC with defeat for Carthage. Rome now controlled Sicily and the west Mediterranean. Syracuse and other independent states in Sicily became allies of Rome.

- **The Second Punic War** began in 221 BC when Rome sent help to the city of Saguntum in Spain, which was rebelling against Carthaginian rule.

- **Hannibal**, the Carthaginian commander in Spain, crushed Saguntum but realized he could not defeat Rome in Spain. While Rome made preparations to invade Spain and Carthage, he led his army on the long march over the Pyrenees and Alps into Italy.

> ... FASCINATING FACT ...
> At the Battle of Cannae in 216 BC, Hannibal surrounded and massacred an army of over 70,000 Romans, only some 5000 of which escaped. However, Hannibal had no siege equipment and so could not capture Rome.

- **In Italy**, Hannibal was joined by the Celtic tribes of the Po Valley. He marched south, defeating a Roman army at the Battle of Lake Trasimeno, where 20,000 Romans were killed for the loss of 1000 Carthaginians.

▲ *Hannibal's army included war elephants, which were led over the Alps and into Italy where such creatures had never been seen before.*

- **Rome eventually defeated** Carthage at the Battle of Zama in 202 BC. Carthage was exhausted from the years of warfare and forced to surrender. Rome was now recognized as the most powerful state in the western Mediterranean.

- **The Third Punic War** began in 152 BC when King Masinissa of Numidia in North Africa, an ally of Rome, attacked Carthage. After a siege lasting six years, Carthage fell to the Romans. The city was destroyed and the population sold as slaves.

Growth of empire

- **When Rome was founded** it controlled about 15 square kilometres of territory. By the time the Republic was founded, this had grown to about 900 square kilometres. Rome was still a small country.

- **At the start** of the first Punic War, Rome controlled about 25,000 square kilometres of territory, with a population of around one million. Allies added another 100,000 square kilometres and an extra 2.5 million people.

- **By 260 BC**, Rome was the most powerful state in Italy. All states south of the Po Valley were either allied to Rome or had been conquered.

- **Conquered cities** and states of Italy were ruled directly from Rome. A few important men were made Roman citizens, but most people had few rights.

- **The allied states** were allowed to govern themselves and even to maintain their own armies. However they were not allowed to form alliances or start wars without permission from Rome.

- **After the First Punic War**, Rome took over Sicily. The former Carthaginian lands were ruled from Rome, but Syracuse, an independent state of Sicily, was treated as an ally.

- **In 238 BC**, Rome seized Corsica and Sardinia from Carthage. The islands were ruled by a Roman governor, and an army was stationed permanently on the islands to enforce his rule.

- **As a result** of the Second Punic War, Rome took control of all Carthage's lands in Spain. These were made into a province called Hispania Citerior (meaning 'nearer to Rome'). It was ruled by a governor sent from Rome.

- **After the Second Punic War**, Rome conquered the Celtic tribes of the Po Valley. Their land was made into the province of Cisalpine Gaul – meaning 'Celts this side of the Alps' – which was ruled by a governor sent from Rome.

● **Macedonia** in northern Greece was conquered in 148 BC and became a Roman province. In 133 BC, King Attalus of Pergamum (modern-day Turkey) died without an heir, so he left his kingdom to Rome. It became a new province called Asia Minor.

◀ *Roman ruins of Carthage in North Africa. The site was abandoned after its destruction and all its territories taken over by Rome.*

Social crises

- **The vast expansion** of Rome began to cause serious social problems within Italy. The problems set in motion a series of crises that would last for over a century and end with the destruction of the Roman Republic.

- **The army** was made up of Roman citizens and the citizens of allied states. These men served without pay for a few weeks each year, but were allowed a share of any treasure captured during a successful war.

- **The generals** were usually patricians, or noblemen. When they divided up the booty of war they usually gave the smallest amount possible to the soldiers. The rest was given to themselves and their friends.

- **The common citizens** (plebeians) were reduced to poverty. They flocked to Rome to live off state hand-outs. Meanwhile, the richer men became even richer and more powerful as they exploited the wealth of the new provinces.

- **By 140 BC** there were very few citizens who owned their own farms or small businesses. These types of people had long been the main strength of the Roman army and state.

▶ *The Gracchus family. Although the Gracchi were rich, they put the interests of the poor first in their political campaigns.*

- **The nobleman Tiberius Gracchus** saw that the division of Roman citizens into very rich and very poor would cause serious problems. In 133 BC, he was elected to the post of Tribune and promised to solve the problems.

- **As Tribune**, Tiberius Gracchus introduced new laws. These distributed land owned by the government to the Roman citizens on condition that they lived there and farmed the land.

- **This state land** was taken from patricians who had been farming it with slave labour. When Tiberius Gracchus announced he would stand for election again, the nobles organized a mob to attack him. The attack turned into a street battle that left over 300 people dead, including Gracchus.

- **In 122 BC**, Gaius Gracchus, brother of Tiberius, was elected Tribune. He was murdered by the senator Lucius Opimius. Days of bloodshed followed as the supporters of both sides attacked each other. About 3000 people died on the streets of Rome.

- **After the death** of the Gracchi brothers, the patricians changed the laws to give themselves power in Rome. They used their power to make themselves rich and became notoriously corrupt.

Marius vs Sulla

- **Gaius Marius** was a Roman general and politician, born into the Roman upper class. As a young man he left his farm and joined the army. He proved to be a highly talented soldier and after a few years was promoted to general.

- **Marius married Julia Caesar**, a member of one of the oldest, but poorest, patrician families in Rome. Already successful in his own right, through Julia Marius made new friends among politicians and noblemen in Rome.

- **In 107** BC, Marius was elected as Consul, the highest level of political office. He introduced reforms that transformed the army. He promised to introduce social reforms as well.

- **Two German tribes**, the Cimbri and Teutones, invaded southern Gaul and wiped out a small Roman army. Marius led troops north and defeated them

- **Marius sold** 130,000 captured Germans as slaves in 101 BC. He then announced plans for social reforms. Roman citizenship was extended to citizens of states allied to Rome, power was transferred away from the Senate and social handouts increased.

- **By 88** BC, the Senate decided to act. They sent for the patrician general Lucius Cornelius Sulla, who marched an army to Rome. Marius fled, but many of his supporters were executed or imprisoned.

- **Marius was captured**. When the executioner arrived, Marius shouted, "Would you dare kill Gaius Marius?" The executioner fled and Marius escaped.

- **Marius returned to Rome in 87** BC. Many citizens rose up to support him and Sulla fled. Marius ordered the execution of several patricians and their supporters. He then died of a sudden illness.

- **When Sulla returned**, he promised to end the fighting, introduce reforms and bring peace to Rome. Instead he ordered his men to kill 7000 supporters of Marius, then another 4700 who had opposed the first killings.

- **Sulla ruled Rome** until 79 BC when he retired to his country estates. He died less than a year later.

◄ *Roman soldiers with large oval shields and plumed helmets. Marius' reforms provided soldiers with standardized equipment, produced to set standards by government contract.*

23

Pompey vs Caesar

- **After Sulla's retirement** and death, power returned to the Senate. However corruption and intimidation were so widespread that real power lay with rich men and successful generals.

- **The most successful general** in Rome at this time was Gnaeus Pompeius Magnus, known as Pompey the Great. He was the son of a famous supporter of Sulla, Pompeius Strabo.

- **The richest man** in Rome was Marcus Licinius Crassus, who made a fortune by buying slaves, training them to be skilled workers, then selling them at a large profit.

- **Crassus and Pompey** ruled Rome. They bribed or attacked opponents so that only men supported by Crassus and Pompey were elected to government. In 70 BC both men had themselves elected as Consuls.

- **Pompey then left Rome** to fight a series of wars in the eastern Mediterranean. He defeated the rulers of Pontus and Armenia, adding those lands to the Roman Empire. He then conquered Syria and Judaea.

- **While Pompey** was in the east, a politician named Julius Caesar grew popular. Caesar was a member of the Julian family, which was one of the oldest in Rome, and claimed to be descended from the goddess Venus.

- **Julius Caesar** was also related by marriage to Gaius Marius. He was therefore popular with both the patricians and with the poorer plebeians.

- **At first**, Caesar, Crassus and Pompey worked together. Caesar conquered large areas of Gaul and even raided Britain. Pompey stayed in Rome. Crassus went to command in the east.

- **Crassus was killed** at the Battle of Carrhae in 53 BC, fighting the Parthians. Without him to act as intermediary, Pompey and Caesar began to quarrel.

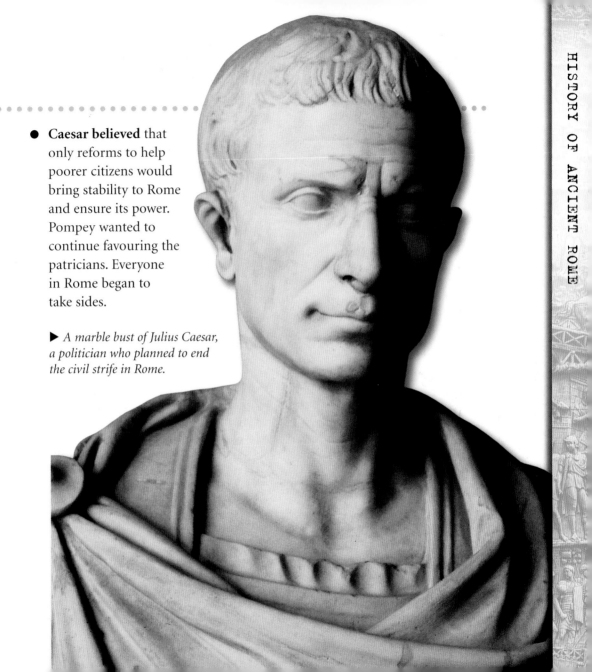

● **Caesar believed** that only reforms to help poorer citizens would bring stability to Rome and ensure its power. Pompey wanted to continue favouring the patricians. Everyone in Rome began to take sides.

▶ *A marble bust of Julius Caesar, a politician who planned to end the civil strife in Rome.*

The civil wars

▲ *Brutus was told by the ghost of Caesar that they would 'meet at Philippi'. Brutus was killed there in battle a few months later.*

- **In 49** BC, Julius Caesar was declared to be an enemy of Rome by the Senate, which feared he would introduce reforms in favour of the poor. The Senate then asked Pompey to capture Caesar.

- **Caesar asked his army** in Gaul for their support. They gave it. Caesar led his army over the river Rubicon that divided Gaul from Italy. He reportedly said, "*Alea jacta est,*" which translates as 'the die is cast', meaning that he had taken a step that he could not undo.

- **Pompey was taken by surprise**. He had a few soldiers in Italy, but most of the men loyal to him were in Spain and the eastern Mediterranean. He left a few garrisons in Italy, then went to Greece.

- **After defeating** Pompey's garrisons in Italy, Caesar led his army to Greece. At the Battle of Pharsalus on 9 August 48 BC, Pompey was defeated. He fled to Egypt, but was murdered by King Ptolemy XIII.

....FASCINATING FACT...
When Caesar arrived in Egypt he had King Ptolemy XIII killed and put the dead king's sister Cleopatra on the throne. Caesar and Cleopatra had a son together.

- **Caesar returned** to Rome and offered a free pardon to all supporters of Pompey, as long as they surrendered at once. Most did, but Pompey's sons raised a new army in Spain. Caesar defeated them at Munda in March 45 BC.

- **In 45 BC**, Caesar began reforming the government of Rome. But when he had himself declared Dictator for Life, many people feared that he wanted to become king. Even some close supporters turned against Caesar.

- **On 15 March**, 44 BC, Caesar was murdered by a group of senators. One of the conspirators was Marcus Brutus, a descendent of the man who had ousted King Tarquin the Proud.

- **A new civil war** broke out. The cause of Caesar's reforms was taken up by his nephew, Octavian Caesar, and by Julius Caesar's deputy, Mark Antony.

- **Brutus** and the conspirators were defeated at the Battle of Philippi in 42 BC. Octavian Caesar and Mark Antony returned to Rome to continue Caesar's reforms.

The first emperor

- **In 42 BC,** the three most powerful men in Rome were the general Mark Antony, the politician Marcus Lepidus and Octavian Caesar, nephew and heir to the popular Julius Caesar.

- **They realized** that urgent reforms were needed after years of civil war. Lepidus was put in charge of North Africa, while Octavius took Italy, Spain and Gaul. Mark Antony was given control of the eastern Mediterranean.

- **In 34 BC,** the officials in North Africa asked Lepidus to resign due to his laziness, but he refused. Octavius crossed to Africa with a small army and forced Lepidus to retire to his country estates, where he lived in peace until he died in 13 BC.

◀ *A statue of Augustus shown in the uniform of a senior military office to emphasize his victorious career.*

- **Meanwhile**, Mark Antony had reasserted Roman control over the eastern provinces. He reformed the taxation system and repaired the defences against the powerful Parthian Empire (in modern-day Iran) to the east.

- **Mark Antony met Cleopatra**, Queen of Egypt, and was dazzled by her beauty, her intelligence and by the vast wealth of Egypt.

- **Cleopatra had several children** by Mark Antony, even though he was married to Octavia Ceasar, sister of Octavius.

- **Octavius thought** Mark Antony intended to set himself up as an independent ruler in the east. When Antony divorced Octavia and married Cleopatra, Octavius declared war.

- **At the Battle of Actium** in 31 BC, Octavius defeated the armies of Cleopatra and Mark Antony. Soon afterwards, Mark Antony committed suicide, followed by Cleopatra in 30 BC. Octavius made himself the new King of Egypt, then returned to Rome.

- **In 27 BC**, Octavius surrendered all his formal powers to the Senate and people of Rome. He said that the ancient Republic had been restored. In fact, he kept all real power informally in his own hands.

- **Octavius took** two new titles. He called himself Augustus, meaning 'exalted one,' and it is by this name that he is best known. He also called himself *Imperator*, meaning 'commander'.

The early emperors

▲ *Julius Caesar died in 44 BC. His name was taken by all future emperors of Rome, including his adopted son and heir, Augustus.*

- **Augustus** was the first Emperor of Rome and ruled from 27 BC–AD 14. He completed the reform of the government of the empire and erected many new public buildings.

- **Augustus pushed** the Roman frontier to the river Danube and the river Rhine, and defeated the Parthians in the east. However, an invasion of Germany in AD 9, ended in disaster when three legions led by Quintilius Varus were wiped out.

- **Augustus' two grandsons** died before him, so he named his stepson, Tiberius, as his successor. Tiberius was a successful soldier and scholar, but he disliked ceremony and did not enjoy the public role of emperor.

- **Tiberius retired** from ruling in 26 AD. He appointed talented men to be governors and senior officials. However, Tiberius could be cruel, and he ordered the execution of several senators whom he suspected did not support him.

▶ *Nero was a talented artist and scholar, but a poor ruler. When he was murdered, the line of emperors from the family of Julius Caesar ended.*

- **When Tiberius died** in AD 37, he was succeeded by his great nephew, Gaius Ceasar Germanicus, who is better known as Caligula, which means 'Little Boots'. The nickname referred to the fact that he spent most of his young life in army camps with his parents, and miniature soldiers' boots were made for him as a child.

- **Caligula was talented** and intelligent. But six months after he became emperor, he became mentally ill. His rule became violent and unpredictable.

- **Caligula** had himself declared a living god in AD 40 and began to order random executions. In January AD 41, Caligula was murdered by soldiers acting on orders of the army high command and some senators.

- **Caligula's uncle**, Claudius, became the next emperor. He proved to be a steady, if uninspiring, emperor. He worked hard to get rid of corrupt officials and conquered Britain in AD 43.

- **In AD 54**, Claudius was murdered by his wife, Agrippina, so that her son, Nero Claudius Caesar, would become the next emperor. Nero then murdered Agrippina. Nero proved to tyrant, and a persecutor of Christians.

- **The government** was almost bankrupt by AD 67. In that year, two provincial governors rebelled. Servius Galba, governor of Spain, marched on Rome. The Senate supported him and Nero committed suicide.

31

The adopted emperors

- **Chaos followed** the death of the Nero in AD 68. He left no legitimate heir to the wealth, power and offices that he had inherited from his ancestors. Instead, the governor of Spain, Servius Galba, marched an army to Rome and took power.

- **In AD 69**, there were no less than four emperors. Galba was murdered by his own bodyguards, the Praetorians, who made the rich nobleman, Marcus Otho, the next emperor.

- **Otho** committed suicide when the army on the Rhine made their commander, Aulus Vitellius, emperor. Then the armies in the east made their commander, Titus Flavius Vespasianus, emperor. In December they smashed Vitellius' armies, captured Rome and killed Vitellius.

- **Vespasian** was a tough soldier who came from a middle class background. He was not a nobleman from Rome, but was an able administrator and became famous for applying the law without favour or bias.

▶ *The emperor Trajan was the first of the adoptive emperors, starting a tradition that ensured stability for Rome.*

- **When Vespasian died** he left imperial power to his son, Titus, who died suddenly and was followed by Domitian, his brother. Domitian proved to be brutal and greedy. He was murdered by government officials.

- **After the death of Domitian**, the Senate chose the elderly lawyer, Marcus Nerva, to be emperor. Nerva had no children, so he adopted the able general Marcus Trajanus as his son.

- **The adoption** of Trajan began a period during which each emperor adopted a talented man as his successor. Trajan adopted Hadrian, governor of Syria, to be his son and heir.

▲ *A statue of Marcus Aurelius. He is usually regarded as one of the finest emperors that Rome ever had.*

- **Hadrian** became emperor in AD 117 and ruled until AD 138. He appointed as his adopted son and heir the wealthy senator, Antoninus Pius, who at once adopted Marcus Aurelius to be his son and heir. The rule of Antoninus was one the most peaceful and prosperous in the history of the empire.

- **Marcus Aurelius** became emperor in AD 161 and ruled for 19 years. He was a skilled military commander, talented government official and well-educated man. He left imperial power to his son, Commodus, who proved to be incompetent.

- **Commodus** was murdered in AD 193. The Roman Empire was torn apart by plots and coups from which the general Septimius Severus emerged as the new emperor. His family ruled until AD 235.

33

Highpoint of empire

- **The highpoint** of the empire was *c* AD 160. During this period, the empire experienced a time of peace, and it also grew to its largest size.

- **In the south**, the empire covered the entire North African coast, from the Atlantic to the Red Sea. The fertile coastal areas and inland hills were divided into four provinces that reached as far south as the edge of the Sahara.

- **Egypt was kept** as a separate kingdom owned by the Roman emperor. The vast personal wealth gained from Egypt meant that the emperor was always the richest man in Rome.

- **The provinces** of Arabia, Judaea, Syria and Cappadocia bordered on the mighty Parthian Empire. For most of this period there were few major wars, but the Parthians were always a threat to Rome in the east.

- **The richest parts** of the Roman Empire were the provinces that covered what are now Turkey, Greece, Bulgaria, Serbia, Croatia, Slovenia and Montenegro. The cities in these areas produced great tax revenues for Rome.

- **The areas** that are now Austria, Switzerland, Belgium and the Netherlands were border regions. These areas had massive military bases and fortifications.

> ...FASCINATING FACT...
> The entire Mediterranean world was part of the Roman Empire. The
> Romans called the Mediterranean *mare nostrum*, meaning 'our sea'.

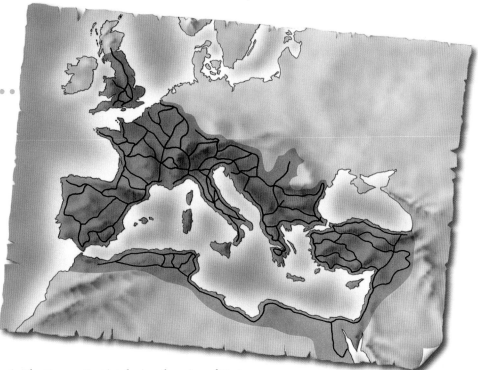

▲ *The Roman Empire during the reign of Trajan
(AD 98–117). By this date most of the known civilized world
was ruled by Rome. The black lines indicate major roads.*

- **The province of Britain** produced crops of grain and wool as well as producing valuable minerals such as gold and tin. Neither the north of Britain nor Ireland were ever conquered by Rome. Garrisons of troops were kept in Britain to protect it from invaders.

- **Gaul covered** what is now France. It was divided into three provinces. Gaul produced rich crops, but had few wealthy cities and did not have many troops stationed in it.

- **Spain was divided** into three provinces and, like Gaul, was the source of much agricultural wealth. Some of the mountain tribes in the north refused to accept Roman rule.

35

Imperial decline

- **In AD 235**, Emperor Alexander Severus paid a massive bribe to the German tribes to stop them raiding the Roman province of Gaul. This so disgusted the legions based on the German frontier that they murdered Alexander and made their own commander, Maximinus Thrax, the new emperor.

- **The new emperor** was the son of a barbarian from Thrace. He had risen to high command in the army because of his talents as a soldier, but he had never been to Rome and knew little about administration.

- **The reign of Maximinus** marked a new stage in the history of Rome. For the first time, a man who was neither Roman nor experienced in government became emperor because he had the support of the army.

- **After just three years as ruler**, Maximinus had spent vast sums of money. New taxes on all classes in the empire made him hugely unpopular. In AD 238, the tax collector in Africa was killed.

- **The governor of Africa**, Marcus Antonius Gordianus, announced that he was the new emperor. He and his son were killed by forces loyal to Maximinus 20 days later.

▼ *The Roman mob could overpower emperors. In AD 69 Emperor Vitellius was murdered by an angry crowd.*

● **Meanwhile**, the Senate announced that Maximinus was no longer emperor. They elected two noblemen, Decius Balbinus and Marcus Pupienus, to rule instead.

● **The plebeians** refused to accept Balbinus and Pupienus. They elected Marcus Antonius Gordianus, grandson of the man killed in Africa. The Praetorian Guard declared for Gordian, then Maximinus was killed by his own officers.

● **The plots**, rebellions and murders continued. In just 50 years, Rome had 24 emperors. There were about 20 other men who began rebellions, which failed. For 15 years from AD 260, Gaul and Britain refused to be ruled from Rome, but had their own 'emperors'.

● **While generals and senators** fought for control, the empire was in decline. The economy failed and poverty was common. Provinces were lost in the east, and those to the north were raided by barbarians.

● **In AD 284**, Emperor Numerian was murdered by Aper, commander of the Praetorian Guard. Soldiers killed Aper and elected the general Diocletian as emperor.

The Tetrarchy

- **At the time** that he became emperor in AD 284, Diocletian seemed to be just another ambitious general. Nobody expected his reign to last very long.

- **Diocletian's first move** was to keep in office most of the officials who had served the previous emperor, Numerian. He announced that he would give positions to the person who was best able to do the job.

- **Diocletian's second move** was even more of a surprise to the Romans. He announced that he was making his friend and second in command, Maximianus, an emperor as well. Maximianus would rule in the west and Diocletian would rule in the east.

- **Maximianus accepted** that he was the junior emperor and never tried to oust Diocletian. The two men worked well together to try to solve the many problems facing the Roman Empire.

- **In AD 287**, Diocletian announced that he was a son of the god Jupiter and that Maximianus was a son of Hercules. The emperors were trying to inspire loyalty and respect.

- **In AD 293**, Diocletian and Maximianus introduced a radical new arrangement that became known as the Tetrarchy, or the Rule of Four. It was an attempt to recreate the peaceful years of the adopted emperors.

- **The successful general**, Julius Constantius, was adopted as son and heir by Maximianus, whose daughter he married. Meanwhile, Diocletian adopted another popular commander, Galerius, and married him to his daughter.

- **Galerius and Constantius** were each given the title of Caesar, indicating that they were junior to the emperors, but held some of their powers.

- **Diocletian** then reorganized the empire. He split it in half – east and west – and divided each province into two or more smaller provinces, and grouped them into 12 dioceses. The civilian government was in the hands of the provincial governors. The army was controlled by the emperors and caesars.

- **In AD 305**, Diocletian and Maximianus stood down as emperors. The two caesars became emperors, and each adopted a new caesar as his deputy and heir.

▶ *The Tetrarchy, or rule by four men, restored order in the empire. This statue shows Diocletian and Maximianus on the left with Galerius and Constantius on the right.*

Division of empire

- **The Tetrarchy** did not survive long after the abdication of Diocletian. Soon rival factions within the army would cause new civil wars.

- **Constantius was given** as his new caesar in the west, a man named Severus, who was close friends with Galerius, the new emperor in the east. Neither Constantius or his officers really trusted Severus.

- **In AD 306**, Constantius died at York, in Britain, while preparing a campaign against the barbarian Picts of northern Britain. His army at once appointed his son Constantine to be the new emperor.

▲ *Constantine the Great unified the empire under his sole rule.*

- **Galerius told Constantine** that he could be the new Caesar, but not the new emperor. Then Severus was defeated and killed by an army raised by Maxentius, son of Maximian.

- **Maxentius announced** that he was the new emperor in the west. Constantine accepted this and married Fausta, daughter of Maxentius. In AD 312, Constantine marched his army on Rome to attack his new father-in-law.

- **Constantine and Maxentius** met at the Battle of the Milvian Bridge in AD 312. Maxentius was killed and Constantine became sole ruler in the west.

- **In AD 324,** Constantine led a great army to invade the eastern half of the empire. He defeated Emperor Licinius at the Battle of Hadrianopolis, and soon afterwards had him killed. Constantine was now the sole emperor.

- **Constantine** was an able and efficient ruler. He ensured that the corruption and poor administration that had grown during the years of chaos were rooted out, but he did introduce new and severe taxes.

- **In AD 312,** Constantine became a Christian. In AD 324 he banned all pagan religious sacrifices and confiscated the treasures of the pagan temples. He spent some of the pagan money on building new churches.

- **In November,** AD 324, Constantine ordered that a new capital city for the empire be built on the site of the small Greek city of Byzantium (modern-day Instanbul). He called it Constantinople. The new city was to be capital of the eastern half of the empire, Rome was capital only of the western half.

▼ *The Battle of the Milvian Bridge. It is said that Constantine had a vision of the Christian cross superimposed on the sun, with the words* In hoc signo vinces, *meaning 'in this sign conquer'.*

The fall of Rome

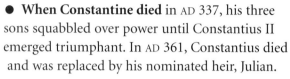

- **When Constantine died** in AD 337, his three sons squabbled over power until Constantius II emerged triumphant. In AD 361, Constantius died and was replaced by his nominated heir, Julian.

- **The emperor Julian** was killed in battle against the Parthians in AD 363. He was succeeded by Jovian in AD 364, who ruled for just eight months. The army then appointed the general Valentinian as emperor. Valentinian at once appointed his brother Valens to be emperor in the east.

- **During this time**, the empire was again in decline. There had been a serious disease that killed thousands of people. The economy began to collapse in the west and became weaker in the east.

▲ *Alaric the Goth captured Rome and stole as much gold and silver as he could find.*

- **From about** AD 350 onwards, the barbarian tribes on the northeastern frontiers became more aggressive and troublesome.

- **In August** AD 378, the combined forces of the Ostrogoth and Visigoth tribes crushed the army of the eastern empire at the Battle of Adrianople (in modern-day Turkey). The emperor Valens was killed along with his senior officers and most of his men.

- **The new eastern emperor**, Theodosius the Great, made peace with the Goths, but allowed them to take over part of the empire. He died in AD 395 leaving his 17-year-old son Arcadius to rule the east and his ten-year-old son Honorius to rule the west.

- **The success of the Goths** tempted other German tribes to attack the empire. In AD 406, the Vandals, Sueves and Alans poured over the Rhine, defeated the local Roman armies and plundered almost all of Gaul.

- **Alaric**, the new king of the Goths, invaded Italy in AD 408. He demanded payment of tribute from the emperor Honorius, but the Romans refused.

- **Rome fell** to Alaric the Goth in AD 410. The Goths rampaged through the streets, plundering, looting and killing.

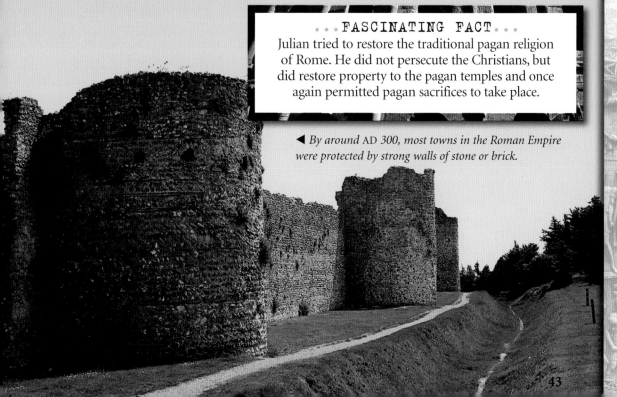

...FASCINATING FACT...
Julian tried to restore the traditional pagan religion of Rome. He did not persecute the Christians, but did restore property to the pagan temples and once again permitted pagan sacrifices to take place.

◀ *By around AD 300, most towns in the Roman Empire were protected by strong walls of stone or brick.*

43

The last emperors

- **The Goths** did not stay in Rome for long after they had captured the great city in AD 410. They moved north out of Italy and then west to attack Spain.

- **The emperor of the west**, Honorius, was safe in the fortress city of Ravenna, but his control over the provinces had been shattered by the fall of Rome. Britain was abandoned and told to govern and defend itself.

- **Honorius** used the wealth of the African provinces to pay troops to try to control the barbarians in the provinces of Gaul and Spain.

- **When Honorius died** in AD 423, power was taken by his aunt Galla Placidia, who ruled in the name of her six-year-old son, Valentinian. Placidia hired the general Aetius to lead the Roman armies.

- **In AD 454**, Aetius defeated the armies of Attila the Hun at the Catalaunian Plains in Gaul. Valentinian, now aged 34, thought that Aetius was becoming too powerful so he had him killed. He was himself killed by men loyal to Aetius in AD 455.

- **The wealthy** North African provinces had fallen to the Vandals, a German tribe, in AD 439. As soon as Valentian was dead, the Vandals invaded Italy. They captured Rome and sacked it.

- **This second sack** of Rome destroyed the city as a centre for government, business or military activity. It became almost deserted and was only used as a centre for ritual ceremonies.

▲ *A pouch of Roman coins. The wealth of the empire lured the invading barbarians as they searched for money and land.*

- **Theodoric**, king of the Goths, sent an army to Italy to try to make his friend Avitus the next emperor. The Goths were defeated by an army of Suevians, a German tribe led by Ricimer, who wanted the Roman senator, Majorian, to be emperor.

- **The title of Emperor of Rome** was now little more than a mask behind which barbarian kings wielded power based on their armies. Nobody outside Italy took the title seriously any longer.

- **In AD 476**, the German king Odoacer tired of the pretence. He told the 16-year-old Romulus Augustulus that he was no longer emperor. The boy retired to his family estates near Naples and vanished from history. Odoacer announced that he was now king of Italy.

▶ *The last Roman emperor, Romulus Augustulus, is forced to abdicate by Odoacer.*

The Seven Hills

- **When the first settlement** was established at what would become the city of Rome, the district was a wild and lonely place. There were no important roads through the area and few people went there.

- **The site** is where a range of hills from the east comes down to the banks of the river Tiber. Seven of these hills would later be included within the city which, therefore, became known as the Seven Hills of Rome.

▼ *The ruins of the Temple of Saturn overlook the Roman Forum. Modern Rome has been built on the ruins of the ancient city.*

- **Three of the hills,** the Quirinal, Viminal and Esquiline hills lie in the north of the city.

- **The Caelian Hill** lies in the southeast of Rome while the Aventine lies in the southwest of the city.

- **The two most important hills** stood close to the Tiber in the centre of the city. The Capitol Hill was the religious centre of Rome and on its summit stood the most important temples of the city.

- **The Palatine Hill** was where, legend said, Romulus built the first city of Rome. During the republic, this was the most fashionable residential area of the city and the emperors built their palaces here.

- **Archaeologists** working in the 1940s near the top of the Palatine Hill found a series of wooden post holes. These probably formed the foundations of three huts. These have become known as the 'Huts of Romulus'.

- **The area between** the Capitol and Palatine hills was known as the Forum, which means 'outside the walls'. At first it was a flat, marshy area, though it was later drained and built upon.

- **Between the Palatine** and Aventine hills was a straight narrow valley with a small stream running along it. In the earliest days of Rome, this 'circus', as it was known, was used for processions and games while the people sat on the slopes of the two hills.

- **North of the Capitol Hill** was an area of flat, dry land known as the Campus Martius – 'the field of Mars'. In the early days of Rome this area was used for army parades and for training young men in the manoeuvres used by the army.

Republican Rome

- **The Romans believed** that the last king of Rome was expelled and the republic was founded in the year 509 BC. They believed that by this time the basic plan of the city had already been established.

- **In fact**, the city of Rome did not adopt its later form until during the time of the republic. The Romans gave credit to the kings for many things that were achieved much later in Rome's history.

- **The Servian Wall**, which the Romans thought had been built by King Servius Tullius in about 550 BC, has been proved by archaeologists to date to around 380 BC. It was constructed to defend the city after it had been sacked by the Celts.

- **Romulus** was said to have drained the Forum to act as a market place for trade. In fact, it served as a cemetery for most of the time of the kings.

- **The Forum** was probably drained in about 500 BC. It was used as a market place and as a route for processions heading towards temples on the Capitol Hill. The Forum became the political and business centre for the empire during the days of the Republic.

- **The Circus Maximus** was was a huge stadium orginally built to stage public entertainment. It was said to have been given its first permanent seats by King Tarquin Priscus in about 590 BC. In fact, it remained an open valley until around 370 BC when some temporary seats were installed.

> **...FASCINATING FACT...**
> The population reached one million around 50 BC. By this time, houses and flats stretched beyond the Servian Wall in all directions.

- **The main phase** of temple-building on the Capitol Hill began was started by King Servius Tullius. This was completed by King Tarquin the Proud and declared sacred by Horatius in the first year of the Republic.

- **In fact**, an early shrine on the Capitol was probably built during the time of the kings, but the large temple that was burned during the riots at the time of Marius and Sulla, was built in about 350 BC.

- **By about 250 BC**, Rome had 100,000 inhabitants. Residential buildings covered all of the area inside the Servian Wall. Poorer people lived north of the Forum and the rich lived on the southern hills.

▲ *The Palatine Hill seen across the Circus Maximus. In republican times the richest people chose to live on this hill.*

49

Imperial Rome

- **"I found Rome** a city of bricks. I leave it a city of marble." This was the boast of the first emperor, Augustus. Rome had grown rapidly, but without planning, for 200 years. Augustus and the emperors planned their building.

- **In fact**, Augustus built only new temples and public buildings of marble. The residential housing was still built with brick as as before.

- **In AD 64**, a terrible fire swept through Rome. About 60 percent of the city was destroyed, including most of the housing for poorer people. Over the following 50 years, the emperors built a series of new temples and squares on the cleared land.

- **Imperial Rome** made use of a new building material – concrete – which they made by mixing ash from a nearby volcano with rubble. Many of the most famous buildings were constructed of concrete, with only the front areas being covered with marble.

- **The Forum** was no longer large enough to hold all the market stalls and shops needed by the Romans. The emperors Augustus, Trajan and Nerva all built new trading areas to the north of the original.

- **The Romans** loved visiting public baths. Some emperors built impressive baths to win public favour. The Baths of Diocletian stood on the Viminal Hill and could hold 3000 people.

- **Between AD 70 and 72**, Emperor Vespasian began to build an amphitheatre in which to stage gladiatorial fights. The vast building was completed in AD 80. This is known today as the Colosseum, which stands in ruins.

- **The huge population** of Rome needed vast quantities of water. The Tiber was polluted by rubbish and sewage so aqueducts were built to bring fresh water from springs in nearby hills.

- **The largest** was the Aqueduct Claudia, built by the emperor Claudius in AD 52. It delivered millions of litres of water every day to a series of fountains on the slopes of the Palatine Hill.

- **During the reign of Trajan** (AD 98–117) the population was about 1.3 million. After this, it began to decline. By the time of Emperor Romulus Augustulus, around AD 475, only about 50,000 people lived in Rome.

◀ *The construction of the Colosseum was began by the emperor Vespasian to stage shows that he hoped would make his rule popular.*

City housing

- **Richer people** lived in two-storey town houses that were built around an open courtyard. There was often a small pool in the courtyard to catch and store rainwater that could then be used for cooking or washing.

- **Bedrooms** were located on the upper floor of the house. The doors from the bedrooms opened onto a balcony that ran around the courtyard. Stairs ran down one side of the courtyard.

- **On the ground floor** were the rooms where daily work was done and guests were entertained. These were often decorated with mosaic floors, statues and painted walls to show how rich the owners were.

- **The triclinium** was usually located next to the entrance to the house. This room was used as a dining room by the family, and was where visitors were entertained. Romans lounged on couches when eating or drinking.

- **The tablinum** was a study. This was where the head of the family kept his business records and private papers. Only very important business contacts or close friends would be invited to enter this room.

- **The kitchen** was located at the back of the house. It often had its own small door leading to a back alley, if there was one. This allowed supplies to be brought in and rubbish taken out without disturbing the family.

- **Very rich families** would have a small garden between the house and the street. A shady walkway ran around the garden, in which grew herbs and flowers. A tall wall was built between the garden and street to stop passersby looking in.

- **Poorer families** lived in blocks of flats known as *insulae*. These were built of brick, wood or wattle and daub. They were often owned by rich families who rented them out to tenants.

▲ *Roman* insulae, *or blocks of flats. People spent little time at home, preferring to meet friends and do business in the streets, cafes and taverns.*

- **On the ground floor** of an *insula* were shops, and on the first floor were flats and apartments for families. These had several rooms, including a kitchen and triclinium. On the top floors were single rooms for the poorest families.

- **The types of housing** found in Rome were copied throughout the empire. People in Britain, Spain and North Africa thought it was fashionable to live in a similar style to people in Rome.

Clothes and fashion

- **The climate of Rome** is hot in the summer with cooler, wetter winters. Most Romans wore clothes that were suitable for living in this climate.

- **The most common item** of clothing for men was the tunic. It had short sleeves and fell to the knees like a skirt. Underwear was a cloth that wrapped around the waist and pulled up between the legs, fastening at the front.

- **Roman citizens** were allowed to wear a toga. This was a semi-circular cloth about 5 m across and 2 m deep. It could be worn draped over the shoulders, or pulled up over the head depending on the weather.

- **The toga** showed the social status of the wearer. Plebeians wore togas made of a plain white material. Senators and their families were allowed to have a purple or red stripe around the edge of their togas.

- **During the time** of the late empire, togas were larger and worn only on formal occasions. This toga was almost 7 m long and worn wrapped around the waist and draped over the left shoulder.

- **Leather sandals** were worn by men and women all year round. The army issued its men with sandals that had nails embedded in the soles.

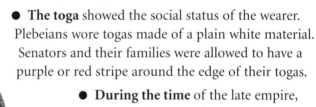

◀ *A wealthy family dressed for a festival. Coloured dyes, such as purple and red, were expensive to produce.*

▲ *Richer Roman ladies wore their hair in elaborate styles.*
Most women had a slave whose job was to keep their hair perfect.

- **Women usually wore** a tunic, but for formal events they might wear an ankle-length dress called a *stola*. Clothes worn at parties and social events might be richly embroidered. In the street, women were expected to wear a long cloak that covered them from head to toe.

- **As the Roman Empire grew**, the Romans found they had to live and work in all sorts of different climates. In North Africa, Romans wore their summer clothes all year round. In Britain and Germany, men wore woollen underpants and lined their shoes with fur.

- **Both men and women** wore jewellery. Men tended to wear rings, bracelets and brooches, while women might wear necklaces, earrings and hair decorations.

> ...FASCINATING FACT...
> In winter, both men and women wore woollen cloaks. Most fastened over the shoulder with a brooch, but some had two brooches. Others had a hood attached that could be pulled up in bad weather.

Family life

▲ *A gold* bulla *acted as good luck charm to a newborn baby.*

● **The basis of Roman life** was the family. Most laws and customs were related to the family and to Roman concepts of family duties and privileges.

● **The oldest man** in a family was known as the *paterfamilias*. He was responsible for all members of his family. He was expected to arrange the education of children, the marriage of young adults and to ensure that everyone obeyed the law.

● **Under the kings** and early republic, the *paterfamilias* had to enforce the law on his family. If someone misbehaved it was the *paterfamilias* who beat, fined or even executed them. Later, the *paterfamilias* merely had to report crimes to the state.

● **People** with the same surname were linked into *gentes,* meaning the same family group. The members of a *gentes* were expected to help and support each other. Richer men gave jobs to poorer men or helped to pay off debts.

● **The most important** *gentes* were the patricians who lived in Rome during the time of the kings. These were the Aemilii, Cornelii, Julii, Fabii, Claudii and Valerii. Their members occupied top government posts throughout the Republic and early empire.

● **When a baby was born** it was shown to the father on its ninth day of life. The father presented the baby with a *bulla*, a good luck charm that was often made of silver or gold.

● **The child** had to carry the *bulla* at all times. When the child reached adulthood, he or she took the *bulla* to a temple and dedicated it to a god in thanks for having reached adulthood.

▶ *A rich family at home. The boy comes to greet his mother, but most of the time he would be cared for by a slave.*

- **Marriages** were usually arranged by the parents of the bride and groom, though the views of the couple were sometimes taken into account.

- **A wedding** began with a sacrifice to the gods, then a meal and a procession from the bride's house to the groom's. A dowry was paid by the bride's family to the groom.

- **Funerals** took the form of a procession that carried the dead body to a site where it was burnt on a fire. Speeches were made then the ashes placed in a jar and buried.

▶ *A funeral urn in which the ashes of a body were placed for burial.*

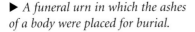

Women in society

- **Roman women** were expected to lead quite a different life from those of the men. Their main role was to work for the good of the family or the *gentes*.

- **Women were not allowed** to stand for election or hold government jobs. They were not even allowed to vote in elections.

- **Some temples**, such as that of Vesta, were reserved for women only. Priestesses of Vesta had ceremonial roles and wielded considerable political influence.

- **Before about 200** BC, women were expected to be under the control of their *paterfamilias*. They were not allowed to own property and could not enter into any business deals.

- **By the time** of the first emperors, women were allowed to own property and run shops and other businesses. Changes in laws had been introduced over a period of about 150 years.

- **Even under the emperors** it was thought to be a scandal if the wife of a rich man ran went to work. It was thought that women should work only if they needed to do so.

- **Poorer women** were able to work without disapproval. Wives and daughters of shopkeepers and craftsmen were expected to help with the business. Farmers' wives always helped on the farm.

◀ *Spinning wool into yarn, then weaving it into cloth, were skills that Roman women were expected to learn.*

- **By the time** of Tiberius, around AD 14, it was accepted that when a wealthy woman got married, she would retain control of any property or money that she had owned before the marriage. Before this date, her husband was given a share in her wealth.

- **One skill** that all women were supposed to have was that of making cloth. Women had to spin wool using a weighted spindle, then weave it into cloth on a small loom that was kept in the private part of a house.

- **A popular social activity** was for women to get together to spin and weave. Men were not allowed at such parties.

▶ *Slaves attending their mistress. Make-up, perfumes and other cosmetics were widely used in ancient Rome.*

59

Education and schools

- **From their birth** until the age of about seven, children stayed at home with their mothers. They were taught basic household skills and good manners, as well as how to count and how to behave in public.

- **At the age of seven**, children began their formal education. But until about 150 BC there were no schools or professional teachers in Rome at all. All children were educated by their own family.

- **Girls were taught** domestic skills such as cooking, spinning, weaving and how to recognize fresh fish and vegetables in shops. They were also taught how to run a household, giving orders to slaves or servants.

- **Boys were taken** to work by their fathers. Younger boys were expected simply to watch, but as they grew older they would be given simple jobs to do and later on, would be taught the more complex skills.

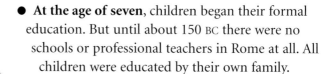

◄ *Only boys went to school. Boys from richer families were prepared for public life by educated slaves.*

▶ *Pens, ink and a writing tablet. Pupils practised writing on wax tablets before moving on to use more expensive papyrus.*

- **In this way** most Romans grew up to work at the same jobs as their fathers. The sons of farmers became farmers, the sons of blacksmiths became blacksmiths.

- **After the Roman** conquest of Greece, around 146 BC, many educated Greeks travelled to Rome, some as slaves and others looking for work. Many of them were employed as teachers.

- **By about 100 BC**, there were many schools open to the public in Rome and other cities of the empire. Only the richest families had private tutors for their sons – most noblemen and businessmen sent their sons to school.

- **At school**, the boys were taught reading, writing and mathematics until they were about 12. After that, most boys left school to work for a living.

- **Older boys** who stayed on at school learnt history, science and rhetoric – the art of speaking in public. Those who intended to become lawyers also took lessons in law and studied famous court cases of the past.

- **All boys** were expected to keep fit and to take part in sports on a regular basis. Adult men were liable to be called up to serve in the army, so they had to be physically able to carry weapons on long marches.

Leisure time

- **Most Romans** worked hard for a living. Even the rich had little leisure time as they were expected to take part in government and to serve in the army. However, there were several days each year when people took time off work.

- **On their days off**, Romans might watch chariot races, go to a gladiatorial contest or go to the public baths. Some religious festivals allowed for time off work.

- **Romans who** could read, would often meet to recite poetry and discuss new works. Most senators, and educated men and women, wrote poetry that they read to their friends.

- **A popular pastime** among wealthy Romans who lived in the country was fishing. A net attached to a pole was used, or a simple fishing rod.

- **Younger men** liked to keep fit in case they had to serve in the army. Most towns had an open field called a *palaestra* where men could practise running, jumping, throwing weights or wrestling.

- **There were many libraries** throughout the empire. Some were set up by the state, others by the rich. Anyone could enter a library to read a book, but the books could not be borrowed.

- **Gambling was popular**, with games based on dice or marked counters being played most often. Some Romans lost all their possessions at gambling matches.

- **Entertaining friends** to dinner, or *cena*, was a popular activity. The Romans thought that nine people was the ideal number for a dinner party. Richer people might hire entertainers such as dancers or musicians.

- **When poorer people** wanted to entertain friends, they would often invite them to a tavern where they could buy food and drink.

- **Children** had a wide variety of toys to play with. Dolls and model soldiers were popular, as were balls and hoops. Poor children had toys of wood, but richer families bought toys made of ivory or metal.

▼ *A wealthy family host a dinner party. Romans liked to eat while lying down on couches.*

Country life

- **During the time** of the kings and for most of the republic, the majority of Roman citizens were farmers living on small farms in the country.

- **Large estates** owned by the rich and worked by slave labour became more numerous after about 200 BC. Some estates were rented out to free men who each worked a small farm on the estate.

- **By 50 BC** there were few farmers who owned their own land. Most land was owned by the rich or the state. However, owner-occupier farmers were more numerous in the provinces.

- **The Romans** introduced many innovations to farming. They developed a plough tipped with iron that could cut heavy soils, and a cart with knives that could harvest grain. They moved crops and livestock around the empire, introducing new strains to many areas.

- **In some areas** of the empire, an agricultural system based on the villa became widespread. The villa was the home of a rich man who owned a large estate, but it was also the processing plant for the estate.

◀ *A country villa surrounded by the fields of the estate. Villas were working buildings as well as homes to the families that owned them.*

▶ *Boar hunting was a popular sport in rural areas. Hunting dogs were used to help catch the boars.*

- **Most of a villa** estate would be rented out to individual farmers, each of whom farmed a small area. Their crops were taken to the villa and bought by the landowner. The landowner then transported the goods to market to sell at a profit.

- **In the northern provinces**, rural people lived a different type of life due to the crops that would grow in the cooler climates. Barley and oats were grown more often than wheat, while apples and pears were more usual fruits than olives or grapes.

- **In Britain** and northern Gaul, livestock was more important than elsewhere. Large herds of cattle and sheep grazed on the lush grass of these lands, where rain fell in summer as well as winter.

- **Britain was famous** for its wool. Sheep were grazed on the hills and shorn of their wool once each year. The wool was baled up and exported to Gaul or Italy for processing into cloth.

- **In Greece and Egypt** local ways of farming continued almost unchanged. Egypt produced huge crops of wheat and that were exported to Rome.

Food and drink

- **The Romans** are famous for eating huge meals of luxurious food and drink. Some of them are quite bizarre, such as larks' tongues or bears' feet in honey.

- **Such meals** were consumed only by the richest families on special occasions. Most people ate simpler meals.

- **In Rome** and Italy, fish and seafood were very popular. Most fish was either grilled or stewed whole, then served at the table. The rare turbot, a kind of fish, was eaten only by patricians and later, by emperors.

- **Bread** made from wheat was eaten in large quantities. Most loaves were round and marked into eight portions by cuts made in the top before the loaf was baked.

- **Barley**, oats and other cereals were crushed and then stewed with water to produce porridges. These were often cooked with vegetables such as celery, leeks or cabbages.

- **Most cooking** was done over charcoal fires, which burnt at a higher, steadier temperature. Meat was cooked on a spit, other dishes were boiled in pots.

- **Meals were served** with several foods arriving on the table at once in a number of dishes. Spoons were used to serve food onto plates, but people used their fingers to eat.

- **Apicius Caelius** was a wealthy Roman famous for his love of good food and wine. He lived in about AD 30 and wrote a book of his famous recipes. Copies of this book, *Arti Coquinaria* have survived.

- **One recipe** from the cookbook of Apicius tells the cook to boil a bottle of red wine until it is reduced by one-third, then add 750 g of mushrooms together with salt, pepper and some chopped coriander leaves and simmer for five minutes. The mushrooms should be put into a small dish for each person and served with brown bread.

- **The Romans loved** to eat pork and ham. Large joints were served at dinner parties, then cut cold and eaten in the days that followed by the family. Sometimes a young pig would be cooked whole.

◀ *Slaves at work in a Roman kitchen. The oven was fired by a wood fire, which also provided heat for cooking pots placed above.*

The gladiators

- **Gladiators were men** who fought in the arena, sometimes to the death, to entertain the citizens and public. The word gladiator means 'a man who uses the sword', though some gladiators fought with other weapons.

- **The gladiatorial fights** began as a sacrifice at the funeral of a rich man. They were held to commemerate the dead man and keep his spirit alive. The first known contest was held in 264 BC as part of the funeral of the nobleman, Brutus.

- **Because all citizens** were allowed to attend a funeral, anyone could watch a gladiatorial fight. Some men realized that they could win popularity by putting on shows. They delayed this part of a funeral until they were standing in an election.

- **Most gladiators** were slaves, prisoners of war, condemned criminals or men who were in debt. They trained for months with their weapons before fighting in the arena.

- **At first gladiators** fought with army weapons, but later used specialized weapons of their own. Theses weapons were always impressive to look at. Most were decorated with paint or feathers and some were plated with gold or silver.

◀ *A Thracian gladiator with his curved dagger faces a Murmillo gladiator with an army shield.*

- **All fights** might end in death as the weapons were very sharp. However, an injured man could ask for mercy. If he had fought well, the man staging the show might spare his life.

- **A gladiator who won** a fight would be rewarded with a sum of money. Some gladiators saved up large sums of money in their careers. Successful gladiators might buy their freedom or become trainers of younger men.

- **Wild animals** were used in the arena. They were made to fight each other or to kill criminals condemned to death. Gladiators called *venatores* specialized in fighting lions, tigers and other dangerous animals.

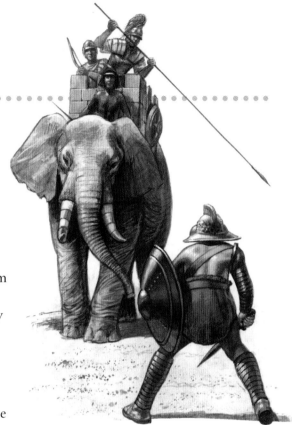

▲ *Some shows featured exotic combats to impress the audience. Here an elephant is shown fighting a gladiator, as actually happened in a show staged by Pompey.*

- **Nobody was allowed** to stage gladiatorial fights without the emperor's permission, as he did not want any nobleman to become too popular.

- **The last known** gladiatorial show was staged in about AD 430 by a Consul in Rome. After this date few men were rich enough to pay for the show, and increasingly large numbers of Christians opposed them.

Chariot racing

- **Even more popular** than gladiatorial shows were the chariot races. People followed the chariot race teams as keenly as they follow football teams today.

- **In Rome**, the chariot races were held in the Circus Maximus. In 189 BC, the small stream in the centre of the valley was covered over. An oval race track was laid out that ran down either side of the covered stream, crossing it on wide bridges at each end.

- **All over the empire**, chariot races were run on courses that were copies of the circus in Rome. The course was about 600 m long and 150 m wide, so the turns at each end were very sharp. Each race lasted for seven laps.

- **There were four** main teams in Rome – the Reds, Greens, Whites and Blues – although there were other smaller teams. Each team imported the best horses and drivers from all over the empire.

70

● **The chariots were** lightweight vehicles with two wheels and pulled by four horses. The horses could travel at a full gallop while pulling the chariot, so races were fast and furious.

● **The drivers wore** a helmet, but no other protective clothing. The reins were tied around the waist, so the driver steered by leaning from side to side.

● **Chariots often overturned** on the bends. So that the drivers were not dragged along by the horses, they carried a sharp knife to cut the reins. Horses sometimes tripped or stumbled.

● **If a chariot crashed** it was called a *naufragium*, or 'shipwreck'. Men and horses would be killed in these wrecks, but they did not seem to happen often.

● **Men riding horses** galloped alongside the chariots. They probably shouted advice to the drivers and tried to stop chariots of opposing teams from getting in the way.

● **Successful chariot drivers** could become extremely rich. One man earned so much money that he retired at the age of 35 to a country estate that was larger than those owned by most senators.

◄ *The most popular sport in Rome was chariot racing. Huge sums were bet on the results and vast crowds attended the races.*

71

The free food

- **Famine was a constant fear** in the ancient world. The onset of a plant disease or sudden bad weather could ruin a crop. If the failure was bad there would not be enough food for everyone.

- **It was a basic duty** of governments to ensure an adequate food supply. From earliest times, the Roman government stored vast quantities of grain in case of a poor crop. It also had the power to force merchants to bring food to Rome instead of other cargoes.

- **One of the reforms** of the Gracchi brothers was to sell grain from the government stores at cheap prices to Roman citizens. Once a month, each citizen was entitled to about 15 kg of half-price grain.

- **This grain dole** was popular with voters. In 58 BC, the radical politician, Publius Clodius, swept to office after promising in the election to make the grain dole free of charge.

- **Many poor Roman citizens** living outside the city moved to Rome so that they could get the free food. By 50 BC, no fewer than 320,000 men were getting the free grain every month.

▶ *Typical food for poorer people included fruit, vegetables, olives, honey and meat. Wine was drunk by most people nearly every day.*

- **Julius Caesar** reformed the dole by ordering a crackdown on men pretending to be citizens, or feigning poverty. In 44 BC, the number of citizens receiving the dole fell to 150,000.

- **Most citizens** took their grain to a baker. The baker exchanged it for a number of loaves of bread handed out over the weeks until the next grain dole. Bakers kept a percentage of the grain for themselves as payment.

- **The poorest citizens** swapped their wheat grain for rye grain. This was cheaper, so there would be more rye given in exchange for wheat. Rye grain produced a darker, less popular bread.

- **In AD 270**, the emperor Aurelian replaced the monthly grain dole with a daily dole of six loaves of baked bread. During festivals there was free wine and olive oil as well. About 1.2 million loaves of bread were baked every day.

- **Government records** of the late empire are poorly recorded due to the threats of invasions and wars. It is thought that the free bread dole in Rome ended about AD 440.

Money and markets

- **Trade was important** to the economy of the Roman Empire. Less than one-tenth of the population worked in manufacturing and trade, but about one-fifth of the wealth of the empire came from this source.

- **Most traders** were small businessmen who made goods that they sold locally. A smaller number of merchants transported goods by boat along rivers or by ship overseas.

- **When Rome was founded** nobody had yet invented coins. Goods were swapped at markets for other goods. In about 400 BC, bronze ingots stamped with a cow began to be used in central Italy.

  - **The first coins** issued in Rome were bronze coins stamped with the portrait of the god Janus. About the year 200 BC the silver coin known as the *denarius* was introduced.

  - **Rome became** a money economy, meaning that people tended to buy and sell things using money instead of swapping them. People could borrow money to finance business ventures.

◀ *A coin of the emperor Constantine has the figure Britannia on the reverse. Constantine was in Britain when his father died and he inherited power.*

> ...FASCINATING FACT...
> There were very few merchants who shipped large quantities of goods around the empire. The largest single commodity, the bulk transport of grain, was organized by the state.

◄ A Roman merchant ship sails into harbour. Trade between the colonies was carried out mainly by sea.

- **During the republican period**, coins were stamped with a picture of the goddess Roma or of the wolf that saved the lives of Romulus and Remus.

- **The emperors** made sure that their portraits and names were stamped on coins issued during their reigns. The other side of the coins had either a picture of a deity or of a famous event.

- **Because the same coins** were used right across the empire, it was easy for merchants to buy and sell goods in different places. This helped increase trade and made the empire more prosperous.

- **After the year** AD 300, the government began to devalue coins by reducing the amount of silver that they contained. This meant merchants no longer trusted the money of the empire. Trade and prosperity declined. By AD 400, a denarius contained one-tenth of the silver it had in AD 300.

Shops and shopping

- **Small family-run shops** were common in Rome and across the empire. Some sold family-made goods, others sold imported goods.

- **Most shops specialized** in selling one particular thing. Olive oil shops had huge jars set into the floor where the oil was stored. Olive oil was used for cooking and for burning in lamps.

- **Pottery shops** were numerous as earthenware cooking pots often broke and needed replacing. They were made locally from local clays and were often coarse and poorly produced.

▶ *The Roman Forum contained several open areas for trading and business meetings.*

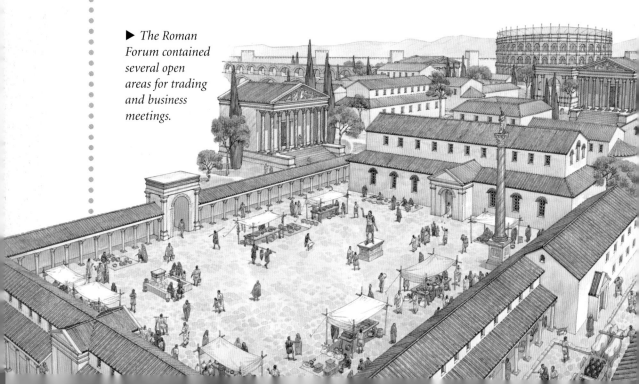

- **Much finer 'samian' pots** were made from fine clays in Gaul and other parts of Italy. They were a characteristic red colour and decorated with embossed pictures of animals or gods. These expensive dishes were used at the meal table.

- **Although women** were supposed to know how to spin and weave, most bought cloth from shops. Wool and linen were the most usual fabrics. The cloth was then made into clothes at home.

▲ *A woman stops to inspect jewellery at a shop. Most shops were family owned.*

- **The largest shops** were usually bakeries. These needed space for ovens, mixing bowls and kneading benches. Because of the risk of fire, bakeries often stood apart from other buildings.

- **Most shops occupied** the ground floors of blocks of flats. Only the finest and most expensive shops were located in the Forum, where they occupied entire buildings, often over several floors, like ancient shopping malls.

- **Markets sold** cheaper goods at wooden stalls that were covered by fabric awnings to give shelter from the weather.

- **The poorest traders** carried their goods in baskets or pots to sell by the roadside. Farmers with spare food to sell in town would also do this.

- **Government officials**, known as *aediles,* supervized all trading. They tested weights and measures to make sure merchants were not cheating customers.

Provincial life

- **The city of Rome** was the centre of the empire, the richest and most powerful city in the world. But most of the people lived not only outside Rome, but outside Italy. These were the provinces of the empire.

- **In many ways**, life in the provinces was like that in Rome. People liked to follow Roman fashions and Roman lifestyles. But in other ways, the provinces were very different.

- **The provinces** in the eastern Mediterranean had been part of the empire of Alexander the Great, king of Macedon and a brilliant military commander. Centuries before they became part of the Roman Empire, they had been ruled by the Greeks.

- **Greek culture** was kept by much of the eastern provinces. Many people spoke Greek, using Latin only when dealing with Roman government. They worshipped Greek gods and lived in Greek-style houses and cities.

- **The eastern provinces** did not absorb much Roman culture. Life in the east bore little resemblance to life in Rome.

- **The western provinces** of Europe, including Spain, Gaul and Britain, had been inhabited by Celts before they were conquered by Rome. The Celts preferred to live in the country rather than in towns.

◄ *A Celtic blacksmith shoes a horse. The Celts continued to live in their round houses and wear checked clothes after being conquered by Rome.*

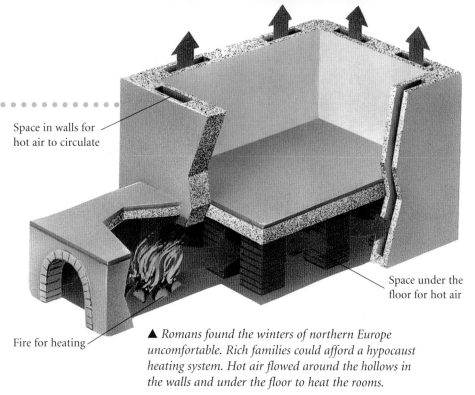

Space in walls for hot air to circulate

Space under the floor for hot air

Fire for heating

▲ *Romans found the winters of northern Europe uncomfortable. Rich families could afford a hypocaust heating system. Hot air flowed around the hollows in the walls and under the floor to heat the rooms.*

- **In these areas** the Romans founded new cities and towns. People who wanted to share Roman culture and be promoted in the Roman state moved to live in the cities. But most people stayed in the countryside.

- **Life in the western** provinces was more like life in Rome, but only in the cities. In the rural areas people continued to live in Celtic houses and worship Celtic gods.

- **However,** all the provinces were subject to rule by Rome. Governors were appointed by the Roman government, and most of them were Romans. Roman money was the only kind in circulation.

- **When the empire** was prosperous, all provinces benefited. But civil wars and decline affected all provinces badly.

The royal army

- **The earliest Roman army** consisted of the adult male population. They went to battle with whatever weapons they had to hand and, as most were shepherds, these probably included slings and javelins.

- **Later legends** exaggerated the size of the army led by Romulus, but it probably numbered about 50 to 100 men. By 650 BC, the Roman army mustered around 5000 armed men.

- **The army** was reorganized by Servius Tullius in about 550 BC. This new system lasted until the end of the time of the kings.

- **The royal army** was divided into five groups of foot soldiers and one group of cavalry. Each group was armed differently and had its separate role on the battlefield. Each citizen was expected to bring his own equipment.

- **The richest men** came equipped with a shield, helmet, cuirass, greaves, spear and sword. They formed a *phalanx* – a dense formation of armed men that was almost impossible for the enemy to penetrate.

- **The second class** of men had a helmet, rectangular shield, greaves, sword and spear. They formed the fourth line of the *phalanx*. The third class came equipped with a helmet, shield, sword and spear. They formed the fifth line of the *phalanx*.

- **The fourth class** came with just shield and spear. They formed the two rear ranks of the *phalanx*. Sometimes, they formed on the sides of the *phalanx*, instead of at the rear.

- **The poorest citizens** were expected to bring only a sling or a pair of javelins. They did not form in solid ranks, but ran about the battlefield trying to kill or wound the enemy with their throwing weapons.

- **On campaign**, the army was commanded by the king. It was divided into four formations for marching and camping, each of which was probably divided into five smaller groups on the battlefield.

- **While the main army** was on campaign, the older men remained in Rome. They had to present themselves each day, fully equipped and ready for action in case the enemy launched an attack on the city.

◄ *Roman soldiers from the time of the early kings. Bronze was used for armour and weapons. Only the richest men could afford to buy a metal helmet and large breastplate.*

Republican legions

● **After the defeat** of Rome by the Celts in 390 BC, the republican leaders reformed the army. The *phalanx* was abandoned in favour of a more flexible battlefield organization – the legion.

▲ *Roman soldiers from about 350 BC. The heavy infantry wore armour and helmets, while the lighter infantry might have wore animal skins.*

- **Each legion** consisted of 5000 men divided into four lines, each of which had 15 units. Each man had to bring his own equipment, but was given a small sum of money to pay for food while on campaign.

- **The front line** was made up of the *leves*, men armed with small shields and javelins. They began the battle by throwing javelins at the advancing enemy.

- **The second line** was the *hastati*. They had helmets, armour and shields. As the enemy closed, they threw javelins then charged to attack with swords.

- **The third line** was the *principes*, formed in three ranks. If the *hastati* were defeated, the *principes* threw javelins, then attacked with swords and shields. The *principes* were the experienced veterans of the legion.

- **Behind the *principes*** were the *triarii* – older men with spears and shields. If the *hastati* and *principes* were defeated, they retreated behind the *triarii*.

- **The *triarii*** were the final reserve. They retreated backwards, holding the enemy at bay with shields and spears.

- **By 170 BC**, Rome would usually field four legions of 5000 men, plus 1200 cavalry. The cavalry were the richest Roman men and could afford to buy a horse and armour. Rome's allies provided additional units.

- **During the republic**, the army was commanded by the consuls. Sometimes, one consul led the army on campaign while the other stayed in Rome. On other occasions, both consuls went to war and took turns to command.

> ...FASCINATING FACT...
> Only Roman citizens could serve in the army. A man could be called to serve in 16 campaigns before he was 46 years old. If he had served 16 times, he was only expected to fight if Rome itself was attacked.

Reforms of Marius

- **By around 120 BC**, the army was experiencing problems. Longer and more extensive wars called for more soldiers, but fewer citizens could afford the cost of weapons and armour. Even fewer wanted to be away from Rome for years on end.

- **In 107 BC**, Gaius Marius, a general who had worked his way up from the ranks, stood for election as consul. He promised to reform the army so that men who did not want to serve would be forced to do so.

- **Marius was elected** to be consul six times. His reforms of the army were dramatic and wide ranging. They formed the basis for the Roman army until the collapse of the Roman Empire almost 600 years later.

- **Marius decided** that the government should pay for the military equipment of the soldiers. This meant that a man did not need to buy his weapons to serve in the army.

- **The pay given** to soldiers was increased dramatically. Instead of being just enough to pay for bread and water on campaign, the wages were increased to be the equivalent of an unskilled worker in Rome.

- **The length of service** was changed from just the length of the campaign to being a full year, renewable each year up to a total of 20 years. At the end of 20 years, retiring soldiers would be given a small farm to live on.

> ...FASCINATING FACT...
> Finally, Marius made the legion a permanent formation,
> not a unit raised afresh for each campaign. He gave each legion a
> number and a sacred standard in the form of an eagle. Rome now had
> a permanent, professional army.

- **Service in the army** was no longer a costly duty, it was a good career choice for even the poorest citizen. Men could earn a good living and comfortable retirement. They might even become rich through plunder.

- **Tens of thousands** of poor citizens flocked to join the legions of Marius. They wanted to serve for years on end so that Rome could launch campaigns far from home.

- **In 89 BC**, the various Italian allies were merged with Rome and all their citizens became Roman citizens. This meant even more men volunteered for service in the legions.

◀ *A legion* aquilifer, *or standard bearer. He wears heavy armour and carries the eagle standard of the legion. This has a laurel wreath around the wings, indicating that the legion has won a victory.*

85

The legion organization

- **The new legions** were given a new organization that would endure for centuries. There were now 5500 men in a full strength legion, although many legions had rather less men due to disease and battle.

- **Each legion** was divided into ten cohorts, each made up of six centuries of 80 men each. The century was commanded by a centurion, assisted by an *optio*.

- **The first cohort** was often twice the size of the others and might be divided into five centuries of 200 men each. Each century in the first cohort had two centurions and two *optios*.

- **Centurions were promoted** through the cohorts, with the centurions of the first cohort being senior to those of the second cohort, and so on to those in the tenth cohort who were the most junior.

- **Each cohort** had a standard bearer, the *aquilifer*, who carried the unit's standard into battle and who dealt with pay. He probably had some religious duties, such as setting up a small shrine in camp.

- **The *tesserarius*** was junior to the leading centurion. It was his duty to post guards and arrange sentry duty. The *cornicen* had a trumpet that he used to pass on orders to the cohort.

- **Each legion** had at least six tribunes who had to be either *equites* or the sons of senators. These officers dealt with the day-to-day running of the legion.

- **One of the tribunes**, the *tribunus laticlavius*, was a temporary appointment. He was a man about to join the senate, who had to serve with a legion on campaign to gain experience. He was given non-combat duties, such as arranging food supplies.

- **The *praefectus castrorum*** was second in command of the legion. His main duties were to ensure that the legion was always ready for action, well fed and properly equipped.

- **The commander** of the legion was the *legatus*. Like the *tribunus laticlavius*, this was a temporary appointment for one year, or one campaign at a time.

▶ *Roman forts were built and repaired by the troops themselves. The everyday work of a soldier involved carpentry, construction and engineering as much as fighting battles.*

Arms and armour

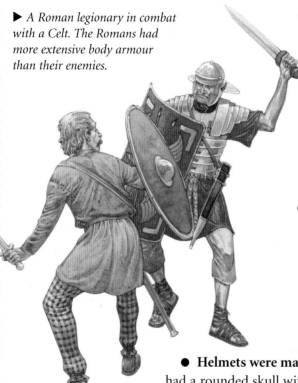

▶ *A Roman legionary in combat with a Celt. The Romans had more extensive body armour than their enemies.*

- **The government** was now paying for the arms and equipment of the soldiers, which meant that all men carried the same kit. Although details varied over time, the basic equipment of the legions remained the same from 100 BC to about AD 300.

- **Each man carried** a large shield called a *scutum*. This was rectangular, but until about AD 30 had rounded corners. It was 1.3 m tall, 60 cm wide and was curved to deflect enemy weapons.

- **Helmets were made** of bronze or iron. They had a rounded skull with a neck flap that projected about 10 cm from the rear. There were also cheek pieces that reached to the chin and flared out to protect the neck.

- **On top** of the helmet was a crest. Ordinary soldiers had long, flowing crests of horse hair that dangled down the back. Officers had shorter, upright crests of feathers. The shape and colour of the crest indicated rank.

- **Body armour** took the form of a short-sleeved shirt of iron mail. This was made by interlinking hundreds of rings made from iron wire. There were reinforcing strips of mail or bronze scales over the shoulders.

- **After about** AD **50**, body armour became more sophisticated. Strips of iron or steel were shaped so that they could be strapped around the body and over the shoulders. This new armour was called *lorica segmentata*.

- **The *lorica segmentata*** was lighter and more effective than chain mail. It weighed about 9 kg, as opposed to 16 kg. It was expensive, so its use spread slowly through the army.

- **Each man** had two javelins, called *pilum*. These had a steel tip mounted on a soft iron shank, fitted into a wooden handle. They were designed to stick in an enemy shield and so make it clumsy in battle.

- **The soft iron shank** of the *pilum* would bend on impact so that it could not be thrown back at the Romans by the enemy.

- **The main weapon** was the *gladius*. This was a heavy stabbing sword that inflicted deadly wounds.

◄ The lorica segmentata *body armour of the 1st century* AD. *This complex design allowed the wearer to move easily while being protected from enemy weapons.*

89

Auxiliary troops

▲ *Most of the cavalry in Roman armies was made up of auxiliary troops, such as these Celts.*

- **Roman citizens joined** the legions. Non-Romans joined the auxiliary units. Most of these were raised from within the empire.

- **Before about AD 40**, most units supplied their own arms and armour. This meant men carried weapons they used before being conquered by Rome.

- **Auxiliary units** were of varying sizes and composition. Some were infantry, some were cavalry and some were mixed. They were recruited for various periods of time and paid about one-third of the pay of the legionaries.

- **Some German units** were made up of cavalry and infantry. Men on foot ran into battle beside the cavalry, holding onto the horses' bridles to keep up.

- **During Tiberius' rule**, auxiliary units were reformed. They were subject to the same discipline as the legions, and pay and service was standardized.

- **Each unit** was a cohort of 500 men divided into six centuries. The centurions were from the same tribe of people as the troops, but the cohort was commanded by a tribune who was a Roman citizen.

- **Auxiliary infantry** wore mail shirts and bronze helmets. They carried oval shields and were armed with a heavy, thrusting spear and a sword. They were trained to fight in a similar way to the legions.

- **Auxiliary soldiers** were required to sign up for 25 years service. At the end of his service, the auxiliary soldier was made a Roman citizen.

- **Some specialist units** kept their native equipment. For instance, a Batavian cohort, from what is now the Netherlands, was skilled in crossing rivers and fighting from boats.

- **Archers were recruited** from Syria and the eastern Mediterranean. They sometimes fought wearing armour, but might discard the armour if they had to move quickly in battle.

Cavalry and horses

- **The area around Rome** had little in the way of good pasture on which large numbers of horses could be grazed. During the time of the kings and early republic, the army had few mounted men.

- **Even in 200** BC the army had only a few cavalry. They were used to scout ahead of the legion on the march, or to carry messages on the battlefield. They were not used as cavalry in battle.

- **Each legion** had 120 horsemen. As in earlier times, these men were used for non-combat duties. They were, however, armed with spears and were used to fight enemy scouts.

- **From about 150** BC, the Romans began to use auxiliary cavalry units. Most were Celts fighting for Roman pay, who were commanded by their own chiefs and leaders.

- **By around 50** BC, each auxiliary cavalry unit had a Roman officer attached to it. He was probably expected to serve as an interpreter, but was also there to keep an eye on the auxiliaries and make sure that they remained loyal.

- **The auxiliary cavalry** were reformed at the same time as the infantry. The cavalry was now organized in units called *alae*, meaning 'wings', which were 500 men strong and commanded by a Roman officer.

- **Most cavalry** was equipped with a shield and lance, and sometimes a sword. From about 50 BC, some cavalry was equipped with mail shirts and helmets.

> ### ...FASCINATING FACT...
> Cavalry armour was often decorated with gold leaf, silver plate and semi-precious stones. It was probably used mainly for parades.

▲ *Carved about* AD *180, this panel shows infantry and cavalry on campaign.*

- **In AD 100**, the Romans met a barbarian tribe called the Sarmatians. Some of these men wore mail from head to toe, and even the horses were armoured. The Romans began equipping some of their cavalry in the same way and called them *cataphracts*.

- **The stirrup** had not been invented at the time of the Roman Empire. Instead, cavalrymen used a saddle that had four leather-covered knobs that could be gripped by the thighs and knees.

On the march

- **When a legion** was on the march, it took up a standard formation and routine that was followed as rigidly as the circumstances allowed, no matter where the legion was. A legion on the march filled about 2 km of road.

- **At dawn**, the trumpets sounded to instruct the men to fold their tents and pack away their belongings. A group of eight men shared a tent, cooking pot and campfire. These were loaded onto a mule and one man had the task of caring for it.

- **A second trumpet** call gave the order to start marching. First to leave camp were small groups of cavalry, who rode ahead of the column to look for ambushes, broken bridges or other other obstructions.

- **One cohort** of infantry was chosen to lead the way each day by throwing dice. These men marched fully prepared for battle and ready to deal with any emergency that might arise.

● **Next came** a group of engineers and carpenters. They were expected to clear any rocks or fallen trees and to repair bridges. The road had to be clear for the rest of the legion.

● **Behind the engineers** came men with mules. They pitched tents and started camp fires when the legion stopped for the night.

● **The *legatus*** and his staff rode behind the mules. They were accompanied by a troop of riders ready to take messages along the column, or to other legions or towns as the commander thought necessary.

● **Mules and carts** carrying supplies, dismantled catapults and other material came next. Inside the empire, carts were used as they could travel easily along the roads, but in enemy territory mules were preferred.

● **The main body** of the legion marched next. These men had all their armour and weapons with them, but were allowed to sling their helmets and shields from comfortable straps.

● **A final cohort** made up the rearguard, which marched fully prepared for battle and accompanied by a few horsemen.

◀ *A legion on the march in about AD 70. Each man was expected to carry his own food and personal equipment.*

Into battle

- **By the time** of the later republic and early empire, the army had developed new battle tactics that had evolved from those of the early republic.

- **The key** to the new tactics was the organization of the legion into cohorts. Each century was formed ten men across and eight men deep. Each cohort was formed three centuries across and two deep.

- **When forming** a line, the legion assembled itself with the first five cohorts standing in a line, leaving a gap the same width as a cohort, between each of them. The second five cohorts stood behind the first, arranged so that they covered the spaces in the first line.

- **The legion** could fight in this chess-board formation. More usually, the second line of centuries within each of the first five legions would march up to form a solid line alongside the first line of centuries.

- **If the first line tired**, it retreated between the gaps in the second line. The second line then formed a solid line to continue the battle.

▼ *The* testudo, *or 'tortoise' formation, shielded the men from missile weapons as they advanced.*

▲ *The Romans could sell healthy prisoners as slaves, but wounded enemies were usually killed after the battle.*

- **Meanwhile**, the original first line of cohorts would form a new second line ready to take over if necessary.

- **When faced by** a solid line of enemy troops, the legion adopted a formation known as a 'pig snout'. The first cohort formed at the front, with the second and third close behind. The fourth, fifth and sixth cohorts formed a third line. The other four cohorts were in a final line.

- **The legion would** then charge forward and use the wedge shape of the 'pig snout' to smash a hole in the enemy line.

- **After a battle**, the general would reward soldiers or units that had fought particularly well with cash payments.

- **The soldiers** could expect to share any loot or plunder that was stripped from the bodies of the enemy, or the proceeds of selling the enemy as slaves.

Fortresses

- **Romulus** fortified the top of the Palatine Hill with a wooden palisade, with a ditch at vulnerable places. By 400 BC, the Capitol Hill was topped by a stone wall about 2 m thick and 8 m tall.

- **The Servian Wall** that was built around Rome in 380 BC, was built with stone blocks. It was 3.6 m wide and over 10 m tall, and stood behind a ditch 30 m wide and 10 m deep.

- **From about 100** BC, the Romans did not build walls around Rome or the provincial cities. They relied on the army to protect the empire and did not want rebellious cities to have fortifications.

- **Most fortresses** were built by, and for, the army. Hundreds of fortified bases were built across the empire, and several remain standing in various degrees of ruin.

- **When marching** through enemy territory, a Roman unit always built a temporary fortification for the night. This consisted of a square enclosure surrounded by a ditch, and a wooden fence about 1.4 m tall.

- **On routes** through provinces where enemy raiders might appear, the army built marching camps about 20 km, one day's march, apart. These could hold an entire legion. They had deeper ditches and proper wooden walls.

- **Stone forts were** built to guard permanent legionary bases and supply depots. These had walls up to 3 m thick and 10 m tall. There were usually towers at intervals along the walls on which catapults or ballistas were placed.

- **In some areas**, the stone walls were reinforced with layers of brick. Some walls were built almost entirely of brick.

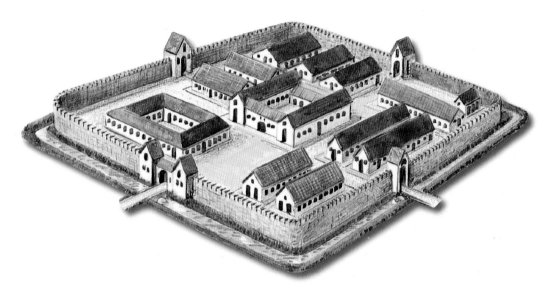

▼ *A permanent Roman fortress surrounded by stone walls and towers. The barracks and store rooms inside might be built of wood or brick.*

- **Gates were** protected by one or two towers and sometimes passed through a massive gatehouse. About the year 200 BC, the Romans invented the portcullis, which could be dropped down to block a gateway.

- **In AD 275**, the emperor Aurelian built a new wall around Rome as barbarian attacks on the empire became more serious. The new wall was 18 km long and had 381 towers. It remained the main defence around Rome until it was breached in a siege in 1870.

Frontier walls

- **The Roman Empire** reached its largest size around AD 116, during the rule of Emperor Trajan. After this, the government stopped looking for new conquests and began to exploit what it already had.

- **The army** was no longer needed to fight against powerful enemies, or to invade and conquer new lands. Instead, it defended the existing empire.

- **The best-known** and best-preserved frontier defence is Hadrian's Wall in northern Britain. It was built after Emperor Hadrian visited Britain in AD 122 and decided not to attempt to conquer the Picts to the north.

- **Hadrian's Wall** runs for 117 km from sea to sea. It was 2–3 m wide and stood about 5 m tall. A walkway along the top was protected by battlements facing north toward the barbarians.

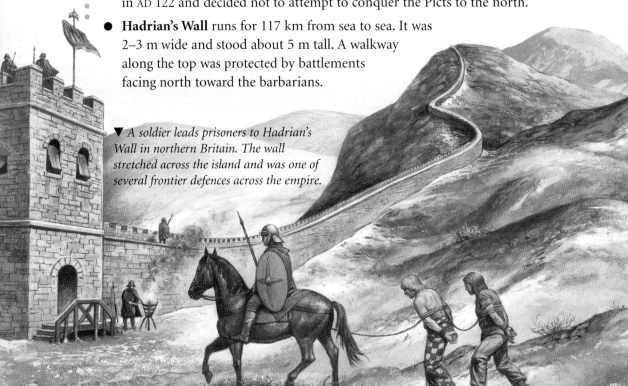

▼ *A soldier leads prisoners to Hadrian's Wall in northern Britain. The wall stretched across the island and was one of several frontier defences across the empire.*

▶ *The ruins of Hadrian's Wall. The square walled area in the foreground marks the site of a mile castle, where soldiers sheltered while on duty.*

- **At intervals** of 500 m, there were small turrets in which sentries could shelter from the weather and eat their food. Every 1.5 km were small forts where 20 men or so could live, cook and sleep.

- **In front of the wall** was a defensive ditch about 8 m wide and 3 m deep. Behind the wall was a second ditch that marked out the military zone in which only soldiers were allowed.

- **The garrisons** of Hadrian's Wall lived in 16 forts built on, or just south of, the wall itself. From there, they manned the wall and went out on patrol in the untamed lands beyond, to keep a lookout for trouble.

- **The rivers Rhine and Danube** were also fortified. Along the Roman bank was a string of small forts and watchtowers, each within sight of the next.

- **Big fortresses** were built close to the Rhine and Danube. These were bases from which the legions could march to man watchtowers and patrol rivers.

- **Only in Syria** and its surrounding areas, where the Romans faced the Parthian Empire, were cities and towns fortified. Here, the Romans relied on the cities holding out against attack, until an army could be marched up to fight a battle and drive off the attackers.

Early warships

- **During the time** of the kings and the early republic, Rome did not have a navy. All her wars were fought on land and the state had no merchant ships to protect.

- **After about 340** BC, the Romans needed warships to protect their merchant ships and to transport armies. Rome used fleets belonging to her allies among the Greek cities of southern Italy.

- **It was not until** the First Punic War that Rome realized that it needed a fleet of its own. According to legend, the Romans copied a Carthaginian ship that ran ashore, but they probably also hired shipbuilders from their allies.

- **All warships** at this time were galleys. These were lightly built ships that were powered by oars in battle and on most journeys. They sat low in the water and had a ram at the front with which they could hole and sink enemy ships.

- **The first Roman fleet** had 100 *quinquereme* ships. These ships had two banks of oars on each side, making a total of 120 oars. The lower oars were pulled by two men, the upper by three men. The ships were about 35 m long and 5 m wide.

- **The Romans were not** such good mariners as the Carthaginians, and lost battles to the more nimble enemy ships and crews. The Romans countered this by inventing the *corvus*.

- **The *corvus*** was a gangway that had a long spike on one end and was lifted above the deck by a crane. When a Roman ship got close to a Carthaginian ship, the *corvus* was dropped so that the spike pierced the enemy deck. Then Roman soldiers poured across to capture the enemy ship.

- **The Romans defeated** the Carthaginian navy using the *corvus*. At the Battle of Ecnomus in 256 BC, the Romans lost 24 ships, while the Carthaginians lost 94 ships, most captured by Romans using the *corvus*.

- **By 100 BC**, the Romans had invented the *dekares* ship. This was 45 m long and 12 m wide, and was much more stable in the water than the earlier *quinquereme*. It had two banks of oars on each side, each oar pulled by five men.

  - **The naval battles** of the civil wars were fought mostly between fleets of *dekares*. At the Battle of Actium in 31 BC, Mark Antony had 480 such ships and Octavius Caesar, 400. The battle was won by Octavius.

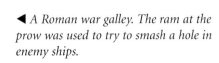

Ram

◀ *A Roman war galley. The ram at the prow was used to try to smash a hole in enemy ships.*

Later warships

- **After the end** of the civil wars of the 1st century BC, the Roman navy had no organized fleet left to fight. It no longer needed the large *dekares* or *quinquereme* warships.

- **The new naval** enemies of Rome were tribal fleets from Germany and the Black Sea, or pirates based in small harbours around the Mediterranean.

- **To face these** new enemies, the Roman navy needed plenty of small, fast warships that could patrol the seas, then move quickly to attack any pirates that came into sight.

- **The first** purpose-built pirate chaser was the *liburnian*, a ship developed in the 1st century AD. It was a slightly larger version of a ship used by pirates in the Adriatic Sea.

- **The *liburnian*** was about 35 m long and 3.8 m wide. It had 120 rowers, each pulling on a single oar. The oars were arranged with 60 on each side, on two banks.

- **Ships operating** in the North Sea formed the *Classis Britannica*, or 'British fleet', based in ports in southern Britain and northern Gaul. These ships often had a large wooden wolf's head carved on the stern.

- **One type of ship** that was present in large numbers in the *Classis Britannica* was the short *bireme*. This ship was 20 m long and 5 m wide. It was powered by 50 rowers, each pulling a single oar.

- **These short *biremes*** had oarports almost 2 m above the sea surface. They were fairly stubby in shape and had bows and sterns that were built up high. This allowed them to cope with larger waves than the Mediterranean ships.

- **The Romans developed** special craft to carry military supplies along the Rhine and Danube. These cargo ships were 20 m long and 6 m wide. They were powered by 20 oarsmen sitting in a single bank of ten oars each side.

- **The river ships** were protected against attack by special fast-rowing boats that carried a number of soldiers. These travelled with the cargo ships.

◄ *If the ram proved ineffective, Roman ships carried soldiers to hurl javelins at the enemy or even to board the opponent's ships.*

Mercenaries

- **Throughout their history**, the Romans used soldiers drawn from outside Roman territory. They formed alliances with states they had things in common with. Some alliances were for specific wars, others were more long term.

- **Mercenaries** are not allies. They are soldiers who fight for pay without regard for whether their own nation or state approves or not. They are usually hired for a fixed term for a set payment.

- **The Romans** usually hired mercenaries who had a specialized skill to offer. They hired slingers from Crete, cavalry from Gaul and archers from Syria.

▼ *Roman relief of mercenaries. Many states hired specialist soldiers that they lacked. States in mountainous areas would hire formations of cavalry as they lacked good pasture on which to graze their own horses.*

...FASCINATING FACT...
The German mercenaries spoke little or no Latin, so they
were unlikely to be tempted to join an internal Roman rebellion
or uprising. Just in case, they were led by Roman officers
loyal to the emperor.

- **By AD 50**, all the areas that Rome had traditionally recruited mercenaries from were part of the empire. Rome raised these specialist units as auxiliaries instead of mercenaries.

- **A few small forces** of Germans were hired as mercenaries in the 1st century AD. They were used over the following two centuries to guard supply lines and other secondary duties.

- **In AD 312**, Emperor Constantine had a bodyguard made up of German mercenaries. These men were paid personally by Constantine and were totally loyal to him.

- **Constantine** recruited several more units of German mercenaries. They were equipped with Roman weapons and were trained to fight in the style of the legions.

- **Later emperors** followed the lead set by Constantine. They found that the Germans were easy to recruit in return for regular payments, and they were loyal to whoever was paying them.

- **By AD 350**, men in Italy, Gaul, Spain and Britain were choosing to pay higher taxes, instead of serving in the army. The money was used to hire more German mercenaries.

The later field army

- **In AD 260**, the Roman army in the east, led by Emperor Valerian in person, was defeated by an invading army of Persians under their ruler, Shapur. Valerian was captured and kept as a slave.

- **The new emperor** was Gallienus, son of Valerian. He began a thorough reform of the Roman army that was continued by his successors, Claudius II and Aurelian.

- **Gallienus realized** that the Romans could not hold the frontiers of the empire. The Persians and European barbarians could too easily mass a force at one point to cross the frontier and raid a section of the empire before retreating.

  - **Instead**, the lands close to the frontier were densely filled with fortified towns, river crossings and supply depots. These were garrisoned with detachments of the Roman legions.

    - **Meanwhile**, Gallienus created a mobile field army that was based at just a few key garrisons deep inside the empire. This was made up of the best troops, many of them cavalry, and had fast-moving supply columns.

      - **The new strategy** was to allow barbarians to cross the frontier, but to deny them the opportunity to pillage towns or to capture supplies, both of which were defended by walls and forts.

◀ *A cavalry officer form about* AD 350.
He has a small shield and long, slashing sword.

- **Meanwhile**, the mobile field army would move at high speed to intercept the barbarians. Hopefully, the field army would arrive in time to meet and defeat the barbarian invaders.

- **The field army** would then march across the frontier into the lands of the invading barbarians. They would destroy farms, kill civilians and devastate the lands so thoroughly that other tribes would hesitate to attack the empire.

- **The field army** was kept under the personal control of the emperor, or of one of his most trusted supporters. This not only meant it would react quickly to barbarian attack, but was unlikely to be used as part of a rebellion.

- **The new system** was fully developed by AD 350. The barbarians were contained and the empire appeared to be safe.

▼ *Roman defensive walls were well built, and were often repaired and reused for centuries. They helped to fortify towns that were vulnerable to barbarian attacks.*

The barbarian army

- **During the 4th century** AD, a new system of recruiting German mercenaries was used. This was known as the *federati*, and the Germans recruited in this way were *federates*.

- *Federates* were given an area of Roman territory on which to settle. They were allowed to live by their own laws, under the rule of their own chiefs. In return, they supplied a set number of men armed and ready to fight.

- **At first**, only small groups of Germans were recruited as *federates*. They settled in rural areas, and the system worked well. Most were used for garrison duty.

- **In the** AD **360s**, the Huns, a new tribe of barbarians from Asia, began to push the Goths, and other Germanic tribes, towards the empire. Desperate to escape, the Goths asked if they could enter the empire as *federates*.

- **The emperor Valens**, fighting a war in Persia, agreed. The Goths were given lands in the Danube basin. Tens of thousands settled on Roman lands.

- **The local Roman** landowners and farmers disliked giving up land to the Goths. Local government officials tried to get the Goths to pay Roman-style taxes. The Goths rebelled.

- **In** AD **378**, Valens led the field army against the Goths. At the Battle of Adrianople, the Goths massacred the field army and killed Valens, who attacked without waiting for his cavalry to arrive.

- **The Goths** were quickly appeased by the new emperor, Theodosius I, who gave them money and more land.

- **Meanwhile,** a new field army had to be recruited to face the Huns and the Persians. The only source of large numbers of men were the Germanic tribes. Vast numbers were hired as mercenaries, or as *federates*.

◄ *The destruction of Roman towns and cities caused economic problems that made it impossible for the empire to pay the army.*

...FASCINATING FACT...
By AD 400, most of the soldiers in the 'Roman' army were Germans. Seventy years later, the Roman government was no longer able to pay them. The Roman army ceased to exist.

The kings of Rome

- **The system of government** under the kings of Rome is unclear. The Romans liked to claim that many features of government dated back to the time of the kings to make them appear older and more prestigious than they actually were.

- **The earliest kings** – Romulus and Numa Pompilius – ruled over a small state. They probably ruled directly, issuing orders and ensuring that they were carried out themselves.

▼ *The kings of Rome were in charge of religious ritual and ceremonies. The earliest Roman temples did not survive, but they probably had a sacred building in which rituals were carried out, as in this later example.*

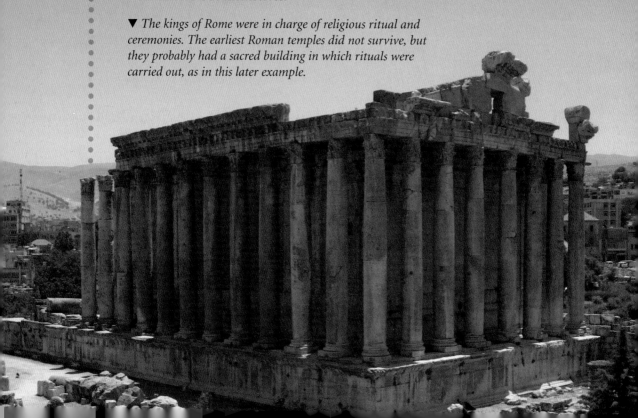

- **Each king** held the position of chief priest of Rome. He had to supervise the other priests to make sure that the correct rituals and sacrifices were carried out.

- **The kings** were also the commanders of the army. They had to supervise the mustering of the citizens, and the selection of those who would go on campaign and those who would stay in Rome.

- **On campaign**, the king was the general of the army. He decided what strategy would be followed, which tactics would be used and gave orders to the various units in battle.

- **When the citizens** of Rome gathered for the selection of men to join the army, they formed the *comitia*, or assembly. The king often used this event to make announcements about new laws or decisions he had taken.

- **The *comitia*** was sometimes asked its opinion by the king. He would ask a question that required a 'yes' or 'no' answer, and the men would shout out their reply. The king made his decision by which answer had been shouted the loudest.

- **At some point** the kings began to appoint rich, powerful or talented men to act as advisors. These advisors met together in a body called the Senate.

- **The king decided** who was in the Senate and what they were allowed to discuss. He would ask their advice, but did not necessarily take any notice of their opinions.

- **In theory**, the kings had almost unlimited power in early Rome. However, he would not ignore the wishes of the people, or his advisors, too often in case he became unpopular. An unpopular king was at risk of being killed or expelled.

The consuls

- **When Tarquin the Proud**, the last King of Rome, was expelled, the Romans needed to devise a new system of government to replace that of the kings.

- **The Romans** wanted to make the government more responsive to the wishes of the people. They decided to create a system of government based on the concept known as *imperium*. The word comes from the Latin *imperare*, which means to command.

- **The powers** that had been held by the king were divided between three people. It was hoped that this would stop any one person becoming too powerful and making themselves king.

- **The religious duties** of the king were given to the *Ponitfex Maximus*, or 'chief priest'. This man was elected for life, and a new *Pontifex Maximus* was only elected when the previous one died.

◄ *The* lictors *were officials who carried a bundle of rods and an axe in front of the consuls, as a symbol of their rank and authority.*

- **The military** and governmental duties of the king were given to two men, who had the title of consul. The two consuls had to decide between themselves how they would organize the division of duties.

- **Two consuls** were elected each year. A man could stand for election as many times as he wished and could serve as consul for as many times as he was elected.

- **At first**, only patricians were allowed to stand for election to be a consul. After 366 BC, any Roman citizen could stand for election, and one of the consuls had to be a plebeian.

- **To stand for election** as consul, a citizen had to be over 43 years of age, and to have already served as a *quaestor*, *aedile* and *praetor*. In an emergency, these restrictions could be ignored, but this rarely happened.

- **Each consul** had a guard of 12 men armed with axes. These men, called *lictors*, accompanied the consul wherever he went. The axes were carried wrapped in a bundle of twigs. This symbolized the power of Rome.

. . . FASCINATING FACT . . .

The Romans dated their history according to who was consul. The year we call 435 BC, was the year of Marcus Cornelius Maluginensis and Lucius Papirius Crassus, and the year we call 58 BC was the year of Julius Caesar and Calpurnius Bibulus.

The Senate

- **The Senate** was the chief deliberative body. It was made up of men appointed by the king to be his advisors, and probably numbered 100 men.

- **Under the republic**, the number of men in the Senate rose to 300 by about 400 BC, and to 1000 by 50 BC. The emperor Augustus finally fixed the number of senators at 600.

- **To sit as a senator**, a man had to be a member of a patrician family, or he needed to have considerable wealth. By 100 BC, this was fixed at 800,000 *sesterces* – about £470,000 today.

- **If a senator died** or resigned, his place was taken by a former consul who was not already a senator. If there were no former consuls, then former *aediles*, *quaestors* and *praetors* would be appointed. If there were none of these, serving consuls would appoint a man to the Senate.

- **The Senate** had wide-ranging powers. It could appoint ambassadors to represent Rome, appoint governors to provinces and decided how much public money to spend on various projects.

- **Discussions could be held** on any matter the Senate liked. The Senate could discuss the actions of the consuls, provincial governors and other officials. If the Senate voted against an action it was difficult for the official concerned to continue.

- **Votes were taken** at the end of a debate. The senators had to walk to one side or the other of the meeting room, then they were counted. If the consul was asking for opinions, he would start with the man who had been a senator for longest and worked his way down to whoever had been most recently appointed.

- **The Senate met** three times a month, each sitting lasting one day from sunrise to sunset. Business not finished by sunset had to wait until the next meeting. Votes were valid only if at least one-third of the senators were present.

- **In the early years**, the Senate met inside the Temple of Jupiter on the Capitol Hill. Later, it might meet in the temples of Apollo, Castor and Pollux. After about 100 BC, the Senate met in a special building in the Forum.

- **Senators wore** a toga with a broad purple stripe around the edge to show their rank. They could also lodge free-of-charge at state-owned farms and properties when travelling outside Rome.

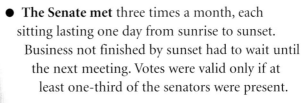

◀ *The formal debates of the Senate took place in the Senate chamber, unofficial discussions and deals were struck in the hall outside.*

117

Citizens and strangers

- **Under the rule** of the kings, a Roman citizen was any adult man living in Rome who was not a slave.

- **After the kings** were expelled, the citizens acquired new powers to decide who should rule Rome. This made it more important for the state to know who was, and who was not, a citizen.

- **The list of citizens** was called the census. At first, the consuls drew up the census each year, but after 443 BC two new officials, called censors, were elected to do this job. The census listed all citizens by name, address and wealth.

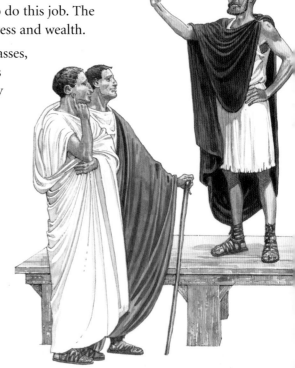

- **Roman citizens** were put into three classes, each of which had its duties and rights within the Roman state. Although only adult men could be citizens, other members of their families had similar status.

- **The patricians** were made up of two groups. The first group were the people who were descended from the six noble families who had lived in Rome during the time of the kings.

- **The other type** was men who were eligible to sit in the Senate, and who were the sons of Roman citizens. These men were usually very rich.

- **The *equites*** were citizens who had a wealth of 400,000 *sesterces*, about £240,000 in modern money. All citizens who were neither patricians nor *equites*, were plebeians.

- **Foreigners** were considered to be non-citizens. They could own property, do business and were free to travel as they wished. However, they did not vote and could not hold government office.

  - **People** who had formerly been slaves but were now free were called freedmen. They had similar rights to non-citizens.

    - **Slaves had few rights**. They had to obey all orders given to them by their owner. They were not allowed to own anything or make agreements with anybody, unless specifically given permission to do so by their owner.

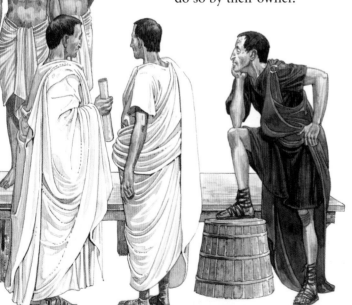

◀ *A slave auction. Roman citizens wore a flowing white toga, while non-citizens wore tunics and cloaks.*

119

The laws of Rome

- **Under the early kings**, the laws of Rome did not really exist. The king was the law and any decisions he made were final. It was the king who decided if a person was guilty of a crime and what their punishment should be.

- **The later kings** did not have time to judge all cases themselves, so they appointed various officials and magistrates to do so. These men decided each case individually as they thought best.

- **During the early years** of the republic, magistrates and officials began to keep written records of important decisions that they had reached. Later decisions in similar cases were supposed to follow earlier precedents.

- **Many magistrates** did not follow precedents, but made their own decisions. There was suspicion that some decisions were reached not on the merits of the case, but to favour a friend of the judge, or even as the result of a bribe.

- **At this early date**, all magistrates were patricians. Because of this, the plebeians believed that they suffered most when odd decisions were made. They demanded that the various precedents and decisions become part of a system.

- **In 450 BC**, the Senate appointed ten patricians to draw up a list of the laws. These laws were engraved on 12 tablets of brass and put up where everyone could see them.

- **'The laws of the twelve tables'**, as they became known, were fairly basic and often vague. In the years that followed, new precedents were set and decisions made.

- **Each year**, the most important precedents were announced by the *praetors*. They were written down and stored in libraries where they could be studied.

- **By 100 BC**, only specialist lawyers could be expected to know and understand the various laws and vast numbers of precedents that existed. Court cases could drag on for months as both sides argued their case.

- **The emperor** Hadrian decided to reorganize the old laws and precedents. His officials drew up a complete set of laws and laid down rules that had to be followed by magistrates when hearing cases. This 'Roman law' remains the basis of the legal system in some European countries even today.

▶ *The Temple of Antoninus and Faustina in the Roman Forum. The Forum was the centre of the Roman legal system.*

The tribunes

- **In 494 BC**, the consuls mustered the army and ordered it to march against the city of Aequi. However, the plebeians in the army marched to a hill three miles from Rome instead, and refused to move.

- **The dispute** that followed centred on the fact that only patricians were allowed to stand for election to office, at this date. The plebeians wanted to be able to stand for election as well.

- **A compromise** was suggested by the patrician, Menenius Agrippa. A new position was created called *tribunus plebes* – tribune of the people. Plebeians could stand for *tribunus plebes* and only plebeians could vote in the election to that office.

- **At first**, the tribunes of the people had no direct power themselves. Instead, they were allowed to inspect all government accounts and watch any official at his work.

▶ *A Roman tribune. He wears a toga over a tunic to show he is a citizen of Rome.*

- **If the tribunes** thought that any official was being dishonest, lazy or corrupt they could collect evidence against them. This was then presented to the Senate or the *comitia* for judgement to be passed.

- **As the years passed**, the tribunes gained greater powers. However, they could exercise those powers only within the city of Rome. Tribunes were not allowed to step outside the city walls while they held office.

- **By 250 BC**, the tribunes could imprison any government official and seize all of his official records. The man would remain in prison unless the Senate or *comitia* voted to free him.

- **Tribunes** were able to supervize the meetings of the Senate. If he thought that the rules of debate were not being followed or that a motion was improper, a tribune could shout out 'veto', and that meeting had to end immediately.

- **The great weakness** of the tribunes was that all their decisions had to be unanimous. As there were ten tribunes in office at any one time, it was often difficult for them all to agree.

...FASCINATING FACT...

The tribunes were considered to be sacred persons, or *sacrosancti*, like priests. Anyone who interrupted them while they were speaking committed a crime, and anyone who struck them faced execution.

Dictators

- **The most powerful office** in Rome during the republican era was that of dictator, so called because the words he spoke, *dictis* in Latin, had to be obeyed as if they were laws.

- **Dictators were appointed** only if the state faced a serious emergency. The dictator held office for only six months, after that time he had to return to private life.

- **A consul** was able to appoint a dictator during the night, but this had to be confirmed by a meeting of all the priests in Rome the following day. The *comitia* could also appoint a dictator, which again had to be confirmed by the priests.

- **Once a dictator** had been appointed, all other elected officials had to resign, except for the tribunes of the people. The dictator then appointed men to take their places.

- **Among the powers** of a dictator, were the right to declare war, lead armies, raise taxes, imprison people and even order executions. There was no appeal against the decision of the dictator.

- **The only limits** on a dictator were that he was not allowed to leave Italy for any reason, nor was he allowed to ride a horse or travel in a carriage – he had to walk everywhere.

- **The first dictator** was Titus Lartius Flavius, who was appointed in 498 BC to deal with a rebellion by some of the plebeians.

- **The most famous dictator** was Fabius Quintus Maximus, who was appointed dictator after Rome suffered catastrophic defeats by Hannibal during the Second Punic War.

- **Fabius realized** that the Romans could not defeat Hannibal in battle, so he refused to fight and instead, concentrated on reducing Hannibal's supplies so that his army was eventually forced to return to Carthage.

- **Julius Caesar** was the last dictator. He had himself appointed Dictator for Life, which destroyed the republican form of government. Caesar was murdered and nobody ever used the title again.

▶ *A dictator wearing armour walks through the Forum. Dictators were forbidden to ride while in office.*

Junior government officials

▲ *A surveyor checks the route of a road that is being built under army supervision. The* aediles *were elected to plan and carry out public building works.*

- **All the elected government officials** in ancient Rome served without pay. This meant that most of the men who held these posts were wealthy enough to be able to spare the time away from their business. In addition, most officials worked only part time.

- **Until about 200** BC, the junior officials of Rome – the *quaestors*, *aediles* and *praetors* – handed out private contracts to men to do work. The officials checked that the work was being done correctly and for the right price.

- **After about 200** BC, the officials had paid assistants. At first, each official hired his own, but by about 70 BC the staff were permanent and continued in place no matter who won the election.

- **The** *quaestors* were responsible for raising taxes, and keeping an account of how state money was spent. They also cared for ambassadors arriving in Rome, supplying them with a house and slaves.

- **The two most senior** *quaestors* supervised finances and kept guard over the state treasury. Two others were responsible for paying the army. After 150 BC, each provincial governor and most generals had a *quaestor*.

- **The** *aediles* were responsible for the public buildings. These included roads, aqueducts, city walls and temples.

- **The two plebeian** *aediles* looked after the roads and law and order within Rome. The *cerialis aediles* looked after the aqueducts and ensured that Rome had stocks of food. The major *aediles* were the most senior. They looked after all other public buildings.

- **The** *praetors* were the most senior of the junior elected officials. If neither consul was in Rome, the oldest *praetor* took over their duties.

- **The** *praetors* **judged** law cases. They decided if a crime had been committed and who was guilty. They also heard civil cases, such as disputes over who owned property, or if a business contract had been broken.

> ...FASCINATING FACT...
> Until 250 BC, there was only one *praetor*, then two until 80 BC when two more were appointed. Under the emperors there were 16 *praetors*, one of which specialized in street crime, the other in legal disputes between foreigners.

The end of the republic

- **The concept of *imperium*** that underlaid the republican system of government, relied on two main conditions. First, the voting citizens were free to vote for the person they thought was the best candidate. Second, the elected officials kept within the law when doing their jobs.

- **The republic** came to an end because both of these conditions were broken.

- **The Roman system** of government had been established when Rome was a relatively small city state, one of many in Italy. By 100 BC, Rome was ruler of a rich and powerful empire.

- **Many of the citizens** who had votes were very poor. They would sell their votes for money, voting for whichever candidate paid them the most. Others would vote for the head of their *gentes*, or his preferred candidate.

- **Other voters** were soldiers, who would usually vote for whoever their general told them to support.

- **Elected officials** were given great opportunities to enrich themselves and their friends by the vast treasures and resources of the empire. Bribery and corruption spread as a few men became astonishingly rich.

- **The permanent army** established by Gaius Marius, was by 50 BC, more loyal to its commanders than to Rome. Generals used troops to enforce their will.

- **Street violence** became more common as the officials who were supposed to keep order, hired gangs to beat up their political opponents.

- **In 49 BC**, all these factors came together in the persons of Julius Caesar and Gnaeus Pompey – successful army commanders and elected officials with enough money to bribe their way to victory in elections.

- **The civil wars** and chaos that followed Caesar's appointment as dictator convinced most Romans that the old system no longer worked. Also, they valued their freedom and did not want to be ruled by a dictator or king.

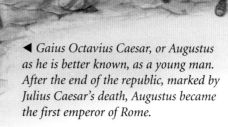

◄ *Gaius Octavius Caesar, or Augustus as he is better known, as a young man. After the end of the republic, marked by Julius Caesar's death, Augustus became the first emperor of Rome.*

The rule of Augustus

- **The system of government** established by Augustus lasted for over 200 years. Even then, it never collapsed completely, but its essentials continued to the end of the Roman Empire.

- **By the time** Augustus had won the civil wars against Mark Antony, there were few people left alive who remembered the time when the republican government worked smoothly.

- **Augustus decided** to pretend to restore the republican system, while in fact keeping most power to himself. Augustus called himself *princeps*, or 'first citizen', but others saw him as the first emperor.

▲ *Augustus commissioned many portraits of himself in painting, sculpture and on coins – he wanted everyone in the empire to recognize him. Many of these survived so we know exactly what he looked like.*

...FASCINATING FACT...
Augustus appointed members of his own staff to work on the staff of each of the elected officials. This meant that he could keep check on what they were doing and how well they were doing it.

- **The traditional elections** of men to government office began again in 27 BC. Citizens were free to vote as they wished, and the men who were elected were free to carry out their tasks as they saw fit.

- **The Senate** was allowed to meet as often as it had done before, and was free to debate and vote on anything that its members wished.

- **There was only one** formal change introduced by Augustus. He made himself the senior tribune of the people. He had all the traditional powers of the tribunes, but without being elected annually.

- **The vast wealth** of his position as king of Egypt, and his massive estates inherited from Julius Caesar, made Augustus the richest man in the empire. He sometimes used this wealth to influence elections.

- **Augustus divided** the provinces into those that were controlled by the Senate, and those that were controlled by officials. He made sure that the officials controlled provinces with army bases.

- **Because Augustus** had such influence over the government officials, he effectively controlled the army. Without the army, nobody could oust him.

▲ *A statue of Augustus. He is shown in a traditional pose used by army commanders when issuing an order.*

131

Patronage of the emperors

▲ *When he was emperor, Caligula spent money to win friends, but was soon almost bankrupt.*

● **The power of Augustus**, and other emperors who followed him, was based on informal powers. The most important of these was the power of patronage.

● **With his wealth**, Augustus lavished gifts on those whom he liked, or who did things that pleased him.

● **Augustus would personally** hand out patronage to the richest or poorest Romans. He would spend as much time granting a loaf of bread to a beggar, as installing a senator as a provincial governor. All Romans expected access to the emperor.

● **Augustus** could usually rely on getting his way when it came to votes because men were so eager to please him. He could even send letters to distant provinces asking the governor to do things – and they usually did as he wished.

● **The giving and returning** of favours was very important. Augustus might arrange for a young man to be taken onto the staff of a successful general, then ask the man's father to vote for a particular measure in the Senate.

● **With his control** of the army, Augustus enforced law and order throughout the empire. This made him popular in the provinces, which had suffered during the civil wars.

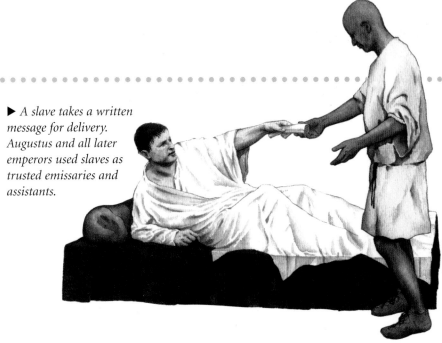

▶ *A slave takes a written message for delivery. Augustus and all later emperors used slaves as trusted emissaries and assistants.*

- **The convention** by which provincial governors had to be former consuls, or *praetors,* was important. It meant that governors had to be experienced, and it provided a reward for men who had worked hard for Rome.

- **Augustus stuck** to the convention, but got around it by having four consuls elected each year. The first pair were nominated by the Senate, the second pair were men suggested by Augustus.

- **Augustus** and all later emperors were the *Pontifex Maximus* of Rome. This put the emperor at the centre of public ceremonies and celebrations so that he was often seen by all the people. The title is now used by the Pope.

- **After the time** of Augustus, the emperor's personal household became increasingly important. Men working directly for the emperor gained great influence and wealth as they could bring things directly to the emperor's attention.

The imperial Senate

- **In the time** of the kings, the Senate had acted as advisor to the king. During the republic, it was the most powerful administrative and body in the state.

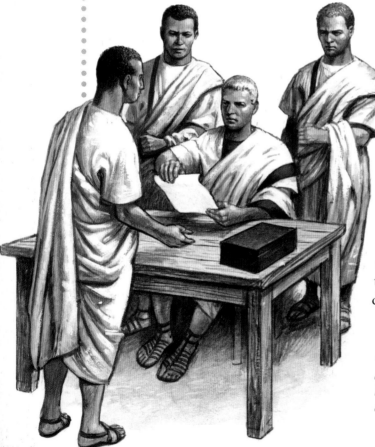

- **During the time** of the emperors' the role of the Senate changed again and again. The Senate was a prestigious and important organization.

- **Augustus saw** the Senate as being his partner in the business of governing the empire. He knew that the richest and most important men in the empire were all senators. He often asked their advice on matters, and allowed the Senate to make many decisions.

◀ *In an election, each man had to declare who he was voting for. Men loyal to the emperor stood by to check how people were voting.*

- **The Senate** was a place where the leading men of the empire could debate and discuss matters of concern. This was a way to bring to the attention of the emperor that there was a problem that needed dealing with.

- **The criminal courts** increasingly looked to the Senate as a court of appeal. If a difficult point of law was involved, or a man was rich enough to seek a hearing, the case would go to the Senate.

- **The governors** and many other officials of the empire, had to be drawn from members of the Senate. These men travelled to and from their positions, spreading news and views among the top class of the empire.

- **By about AD 100**, the meetings of the Senate were becomingly increasingly concerned with the government of Rome and Italy, not the empire. The men who attended the Senate were increasingly local men.

- **By AD 150**, rich men living in the provinces were being made senators as a mark of respect by the emperors. This gave them prestige in their local areas and made them eligible for positions in the government.

- **These senators** from the provinces rarely went to Rome or attended meetings of the Senate. The position of being a senator and the Senate itself, soon had little to do with each other.

. . .FASCINATING FACT. . .
As the government of the late empire began to collapse, the Senate took upon itself the tasks of daily administration in Rome and nearby areas. It was one of the very few institutions of ancient Rome to survive. There is still an elected Senate running the local government of the city of Rome today.

Elections to office

- **When the last king** of Rome was expelled from the city, the Romans decided that the government officials, who were previously appointed by the king, should now be elected by the citizens instead.

- **Elections to office** were held at assemblies of all the citizens of Rome. These assemblies took place in the open air, often in the Forum. Any man who was a citizen could attend and vote, but nobody was forced to turn up.

- **The origins** of the assemblies relate back the musterings of the army by the kings of Rome. At these assemblies the men were divided into the units they would serve in, in the army.

- **This type of assembly** was called the *comitia centuriata*, and it was used when consuls and other officials were to be elected. All citizens were classified depending on whether they were rich enough to serve as cavalry, legionaries or *leves*. Then each section was divided into ten groups.

◄ *The Roman Forum seen from the south. The citizens of Rome gathered here to vote in elections once each year.*

- **Votes were held** within each group. The group leader announced which way his group had voted, and this counted as one vote in the final election.

- **Because there were** always fewer men rich enough to serve as cavalry, those groups were smaller, but they still had one final vote per group. This meant that the rich had more say over the final result than the poor.

- **The second type** of assembly was the *comitia tributa*, which was used when voting on new laws. This assembly also voted by groups, but this time the groups were allocated according to tax-paying districts.

- **The voting** in the *comitia tributa* still favoured the rich, but not so much as in the *comitia centuriata*. During the time of the emperors only the *comitia tributa* was called, and it elected officials as well as passing laws.

- **If a man was taken ill** during a meeting of either *comitia*, the meeting had to be halted immediately and called to meet again on a different day.

- **During the time** of the emperors, only motions, or candidates approved by the Senate, were put to a vote in the *comitia*. Since the emperor effectively controlled the Senate, citizens were powerless to pass laws he did not want.

137

The organization of empire

- **A key problem** facing the government of the Roman Empire was its sheer size. It measured about 4200 km from east to west, and 2400 km from north to south.

- **Government messages** and orders could travel only as quickly as the man carrying them. Even travelling virtually non-stop, it would take a man three months to travel from one end of the empire to another.

- **The central government** could not physically administer the more remote areas of the empire. Any instructions issued in response to events would be out of date before they arrived.

- **Instead**, the empire was divided into a number of provinces, each of which was administered by a governor appointed by the government. Under the republic governors were former consuls, or *praetors,* appointed for one year at a time.

- **The governors** were in control of all aspects of government in the province and commanded any troops stationed there. They acted as the head judge as well as the head of government, and had almost unlimited power.

- **After their year** in office, the governors had to return to Rome. There, they were questioned about their actions and finances. Any governor who was suspected of dishonesty or breaking the law would be put on trial.

- **Provinces** had governing systems based on that of Rome. There were *quaestors* to look after finances, and other junior officials.

- **During the time** of the emperors, the governors were usually formerly elected officials, but they might stay in post for years at a time. The emperor sent officials to keep an eye on governors while they were in office.

- **Provinces that were peaceful** and relatively easy to administer had governors appointed by the Senate. The emperor himself appointed governors to provinces that had armies stationed within them.

- **In the later years** of empire, the governors no longer had control over troops, who were by then commanded by generals responsible to the emperor. Most provinces were divided up into several smaller provinces.

▼ *In AD 43, Britannia became a province of Rome. In AD 60, Queen Boudicca led a revolt against Roman rule, but was eventually defeated.*

Governors and their staff

- **Much of the administration** and government of a province was in the hands of local government, not of the governor. The main job of the governor was to ensure that the province provided to Rome what it was supposed to.

- **The most important task** of a governor was to raise the taxes due to the Roman Empire and make sure that they reached Rome safely. The governor might also have to raise auxiliary troops and send them on campaign.

- **Taxes were usually** collected by private men. These men agreed an annual contract with the governor. They might be paid a percentage of the taxes collected, or be allowed to keep anything over a set amount that was paid to the governor.

▲ *A tax collector inspects his official list to see how much a farmer is expected to pay.*

- **A second duty** was to carry out the orders of the central government. Such orders usually related to keeping roads in good condition, and providing food and accommodation for officials or soldiers passing through.

- **A third duty** was to ensure that the inhabitants of the province obeyed the law and did not cause any trouble. Most governors spent most of their time on this task.

- **Some areas kept** their own legal systems, others adopted the Roman legal system. In both cases, the governor was expected to act as a court of appeal if there was a difficult case or if important men were involved in a dispute.

- **To help him** with these tasks a governor would have only a few men. The governor of Britain might have a full-time staff of only 20 or 30 men. Most work was contracted out so that the governor and his officials only had to check work done by others.

- **The written records** of the province were not kept for very long. Storing paper rolls was difficult and expensive, especially in damper countries, such as Britain or Gaul. As soon as the central government had approved accounts and records, they were thrown out.

- **In the later empire**, governors were expected to write to Rome regularly. They had to keep the central government informed of local events and often asked advice about what to do next.

> ...FASCINATING FACT...
> Important decisions, such as the granting of Roman citizenship
> to a provincial, were usually engraved on bronze tablets so that they
> would be kept more easily.

Local government

- **Throughout the Roman Empire** most people lived their entire lives without coming into direct contact with the government at all. Instead, it was the local government organizations that regulated daily life.

- **The cities** that already existed before the area was conquered by the Romans were generally allowed to keep their own system of government. Athens, for instance, retained its democratic town council.

- **However**, the existing governments knew that their powers had been drastically reduced when it came to relations with other cities or states. Neither Athens, nor any other state within the empire, could declare war or make a treaty without permission from Rome.

- **Although such cities** were free to run themselves, they had to pay taxes or tribute to Rome.

- **Where cities did not exist** before the time of Roman rule, the Romans encouraged them to thrive. Rome had been a city state and Roman systems of government were based on those of the city.

- **Some new cities** were artificial creations of the Romans. The modern city of Cologne began as a Roman colony on the river Rhine. It was populated entirely by Roman citizens from elsewhere in the empire.

- **Other new cities** grew naturally. London was a small village before the Romans conquered Britain, but after the Romans built a bridge there, the village grew quickly to become a prosperous city filled with merchants and traders.

- **Local people** were encouraged to take a lead in local government. In Britain, the province was divided into areas called *civitas*, each of which was based on the territory of the pre-Roman Celtic tribes.

142

▲ *The city of Londinium (London) in about AD 300. The city became a great centre of trade and was the biggest city in the province of Britannia.*

- **Each *civitas*** was administered from a new city. The local landowners and nobles were granted Roman citizenship and expected to play a lead role in local government.

- **Whatever form** the local government took, it was always closely watched by the governor. Some independence was considered a good thing, but too much might encourage rebellion or withholding of taxes.

143

Choosing an emperor

- **The system of government** established by Augustus gave great power to the emperor, but that power was largely informal and took place behind the scenes. There was no official way for the power of Augustus to pass to another after he died.

- **Before he died**, Augustus chose his son-in-law, Tiberius, as his successor. He adopted Tiberius as his son, then persuaded the Senate to give him the same offices and powers as he held.

▶ *Praetorian Guard on duty in Rome. These men, the personal bodyguards of the emperors, were the only soldiers allowed inside Rome during imperial times.*

- **When Augustus died**, the Senate confirmed the powers already given to Tiberius, who had inherited his adopted father's family wealth and contacts. Tiberius, likewise, left the family wealth and position to Augustus' great-grandson, Caligula.

- **The murder of Caligula** meant that there was no official heir to the emperor. The Senate began a debate on a motion calling for the return of the republican system of government.

- **However**, the personal bodyguard of the emperor – the Praetorian Guard – announced that they were supporting Caligula's uncle, and Augustus' grandson Claudius, to be the next emperor.

- **The Praetorians** marched to the Senate and intimidated them into passing a motion giving Claudius the same powers as had been held by Caligula.

- **After the accession** of Claudius, the Praetorian Guard played an important part in the imperial succession. They were all experienced veterans chosen to join the bodyguard for their skill and toughness.

- **Most importantly**, the Praetorians were the only soldiers allowed to be permanently stationed in Italy. They were usually on hand when an emperor died and could use their swords to put a successor in place.

- **In AD 69**, the general Vespasian became emperor when he marched his army to Rome. Even the Praetorians had to give in when faced by a large army of legionaries and auxiliaries.

- **After Vespasian's accession**, most emperors followed the lead of Augustus. They adopted a suitable person as their son and heir, and arranged an orderly handover, making sure that the Senate and army approved of the new emperor.

The army in control

- **After the murder** of the emperor Commodus in AD 193, the Senate voted to make the famously well-educated retired soldier, Publius Helvius Pertinax, the new emperor. Pertinax agreed and was installed in power.

- **When Pertinax** tried to reduce the excessive wages and bonuses paid to the army, he was murdered by the Praetorian Guard. The Praetorians then appointed Marcus Didius Julianus to be emperor.

- **Julianus lavished gifts** on the Praetorians, which alienated the fighting legions stationed on the frontiers. The 16 legions of the Rhine-Danube frontier appointed the general Lucius Septimius Severus as emperor.

- **Septimius Severus** marched an army to Rome. As the troops approached, the Senate declared that Julianus was deposed and that Severus was the new emperor. The Senate sent a small group of men to kill Julianus.

- **Severus' rule** officially started with the vote in the Senate that ousted Julianus, and gave him the powers and wealth of an emperor. However, it was clear that the Senate had only passed the motion because of the approaching army.

- **The commander** Maximinus Thrax, was proclaimed emperor by the army in AD 235, but he waited until the Senate had passed a motion acclaiming him, before assuming the title. When a group of senators objected to this, Maximinus had them executed.

◄ *A general addresses his men on campaign. Popular commanders used their men to fight their way to power.*

▲ *War elephants on the march. These powerful, but unreliable, weapons were often used to impress civilians than to fight battles.*

- **In AD 238**, the Senate once again tried to assert itself. It appointed two highly respected senators, Decius Balbinus and Marcus Pupienus, to be joint emperors. But these men lacked support outside the Senate and were murdered by the Praetorians.

- **The army** rallied round Gordian III, who came to Rome to accept a vote of the Senate to make him emperor. After this, the Senate never tried to appoint an emperor again. They always waited to see who the army supported first.

- **If an emperor** did not win military victories quickly, or failed to give the soldiers a share of their own wealth, he was murdered and a new commander appointed in his place.

- **Even the successful emperors**, such as Diocletian and Constantine, only managed to stay in power because they kept the soldiers content.

Puppet emperors

- **After the catastrophic** military defeat of Adrianople in Turkey in AD 378, the prestige of the emperors among the soldiers was seriously undermined. The soldiers preferred to trust their commander, rather than an emperor a distance away.

- **In AD 455**, the army appointed Petronius Maximus to be emperor and the Senate, as always, agreed to pass the usual motion conferring power and wealth on him. It was almost the last time that army and Senate bothered with such action.

- **Three months after** Petronius Maximus was killed fighting the Vandals, the Visigothic King Theodoric II, announced that he wanted his friend, Senator Avitus, to be emperor. Nobody objected.

▶ *Ricimer was the Germanic commander of the Roman army in the mid-5th century. He appointed Roman senators to be emperor, so long as they followed his instructions.*

- **As emperor**, Avitus never went to Rome. He stayed at the court of Theodoric in southern Gaul and issued his instructions from there.

- **After just a year**, Avitus was told by the Germanic army commander, Ricimer, that he was no longer emperor. Theodoric did not want war, so Avitus was made Bishop of Placentia.

- **Ricimer knew** that the eastern emperor Leo, would not tolerate a German as western emperor, so he did not take the title for himself. Instead, he appointed the noble and respected Roman senator, Majorian, to be emperor.

- **In AD 461**, Ricimer killed Majorian when the emperor refused to do as he was told. Ricimer chose Libius Severus as the next emperor, another senator who wisely did exactly what the German army commander told him to do. Severus died of old age in AD 465.

- **The next two emperors** were chosen by Ricimer, to be his puppets. By this date the emperor had power only in Italy. All other areas had fallen to barbarian kings who ignored any orders from Rome.

- **Ricimer died** in AD 472, and his position as commander of the German troops that by now comprised the army of the western empire, was taken by Gundobad. The new military hard man appointed a new emperor, but both were ousted by an army coup in AD 475.

- **The new commander**, Orestes, put his own son in position as emperor. By this time, however, the western empire no longer had access to enough tax money to pay the German soldiers. Orestes was killed by mutinous troops, and the last emperor abdicated.

Roman architecture

- **The earliest buildings** in Rome were constructed of wood, roofed with thatch. By around 600 BC, brick was being used more widely. Stone was used only for defensive walls and other military purposes.

- **In about 520 BC**, the Romans began to build a new temple to the god Jupiter on the Capitol Hill. The new building was made of stone and followed Greek designs. Soon most public buildings in Rome followed Greek designs.

- **Temples were rectangular** and had roofs supported on rows of columns. Within the temple was a room in which stood a statue of the god. Like the Greeks, the Romans sometimes built small round temples.

- **The Romans copied** three styles of Greek architecture. The Doric was plain but had numerous carvings attached to the structure, the Ionic had more complex decoration while the Corinthian was lavishly embellished.

- **Two more styles** of architecture were developed by the Romans. The Tuscan was similar to the Doric, but lacked the carvings. The composite was an eclectic mix of styles that varied widely.

- **The Romans invented** a new type of building – the basilica. This style was most often used for law courts, but basilicas was also used for council chambers or markets.

- **Basilicas** had a long central nave with a lower-roofed aisle along either side. The style was copied by early Christians for their churches. Even today many churches have a nave and aisles.

- **The Romans developed** the arch, which they copied from the Etruscans. An arch spreads the weight of a building evenly over an empty space, pushing down on the supports on either side.

- **By extending** an arch into a long structure, the Romans invented the barrel vault, an entirely new way of roofing over a building. When two barrel vaults met at right angles, the Romans produced the groin vault.

- **The dome** was a Roman invention. It was made by producing an arch that was circular, rather than linear. The Romans produced gigantic domes so large that nobody was able to build anything like them until the 16th century.

▼ *Romans borrowed the use of upright pillars from the Greeks, but added their own invention of the round-topped arch.*

Building methods

- **The Romans built** massive structures across the empire. Every area was encouraged to erect public buildings, such as temples and basilicas as a mark of how civilized and important the area and its people were.

- **To erect these structures** the Romans relied on human and animal musclepower. Some machines did exist – such as cranes or hoists – but all of these had to be powered by humans, mules or oxen.

- **Stone was cut** in quarries. It was split by drilling holes into which wooden wedges were inserted. When the wedges were soaked in water they swelled and split the rock. The stone was then cut into blocks with iron saws.

- **Because stone** is heavy and expensive to transport, most was used to make buildings close to the quarry. Only certain types of stone with special qualities was transported more than a few kilometres.

- **The final shaping** of stones was carried out on the building site. Iron saws and chisels were used to make sure that each block was exactly the right shape.

- **Offcuts and mis-shapen** stones were used to build cheaper structures. These were fixed into a wooden frame, then pounded with gravel and sand to form a solid mass. This was then covered over with plaster.

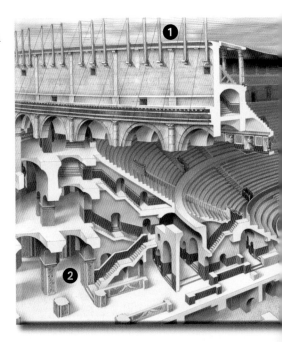

- **Clay bricks** were widely used. They were smaller than modern bricks and made by hand in a wooden mould. Before the first century AD, bricks were dried in the sun. After this date, they was left to dry, then baked in a kiln to make them hard and waterproof.

- **Both bricks and stone blocks** were held together by mortar. This was made by mixing lime with sand, and adding water. Mortar becomes very hard when it sets, and it glued the bricks and stones together.

- **The Romans** were the first to use concrete, which they made with volcanic earth, lime and aggregate (smaller broken pieces of rock and earth). By AD 100, many buildings were being built of concrete. They were then faced with stone or brick.

- **Most large** public buildings put up during the time of the emperors were constructed using slave labour. Thousands of men worked at building sites in Rome and throughout the empire.

Key

1. Wooden masts which supported the awning
2. Passageways where gladiators and aninmals were kept before they went into the arena
3. Tiered seating for the audience

◀ *The Colosseum was a masterpiece of engineering and architecture. It stood several storeys tall, had an awning to provide shade, and layers of underground galleries below the arena.*

153

Water systems

- **The Romans built** effective water systems. Rome itself had an astonishing network of pipes, sewers and aqueducts. Every provincial town in the empire had its own water system.

- **The first sewer** in Rome was the *Cloaca Maxima* – the great drain. This was built during the reign of Tarquin Priscus. It drained the marshy Forum area, but was also used to transport sewage and rubbish into the Tiber.

- **As Rome expanded**, more and more drains were added to the system. Most drains met the *Cloaca Maxima*, but others poured straight into the Tiber. Men called *cloacae* patrolled the sewers, repairing the structures.

▼ *An aqueduct built by the Romans to carry water over a valley in Spain. The provision of fresh water to towns and cities was a priority.*

- **By 250 BC**, the wells in Rome were no longer producing clean drinking water and the Tiber was polluted by sewage. The Romans began to build aqueducts purposely to bring fresh spring water into the city.

- **Aqueducts** were built of stone or brick and could be over 80 km long. Water was collected at a spring in nearby hills, then flowed into a covered channel that ran around the contours of the hills. Where the aqueduct had to cross low land, it was carried on a series of arches.

- **Most aqueducts** ended at a series of public fountains. The water gushed into a large bowl from where people could collect it in buckets, to be taken back to their homes. Rich families could pay to have pipes from the aqueduct to carry water direct to their homes.

- **Some aqueducts** ran into baths. The baths consumed enormous quantities of water, and they needed their own sources that were separate from those of the rest of the city.

- **Public lavatories** were located throughout Rome and other cities. These consisted of stone or wooden seats over a sewer that carried a flow of water from an aqueduct. The water flowed continuously to flush the waste away.

- **Rich people** did not visit public lavatories. Instead, they used pots in their own homes. The pots were carried to the public lavatories by slaves, who dumped the contents down the drains.

...FASCINATING FACT...
Sponges mounted on sticks were provided in public toilets for people to use to wipe their bottoms.

Public baths

- **From the earliest times**, Romans believed that baths were a sign of civilization. Rome had dozens of public baths, and all towns or cities in the empire had at least one. Even army posts had baths for the soldiers.

- **A Roman bath** was a public building where people went to relax and enjoy themselves. Most were built by the emperor or a rich local man, as a gift to the public. They were either free or very cheap to enter.

- **The process of bathing** was complex and might take up to two hours. The first stage was to enter a very hot room, which had a pot of boiling water to fill the air with steam. This was the *laconicum*.

- **After the *laconicum***, bathers moved to the *caldarium*, another hot room with a small pool of hot water for bathing. Next was the *tepidarium*, a warm room with a warm pool.

- **Attendants** in the *tepidarium* would massage the bathers. Olive oil was rubbed into the body to draw out any dirt and impurities. The oil was then scraped off with a curved bronze tool called a *strigil*.

- **The next stage** was the *frigidarium*. This was an unheated room or an open courtyard, in which was a pool of cold water. People might spend hours relaxing around the pool.

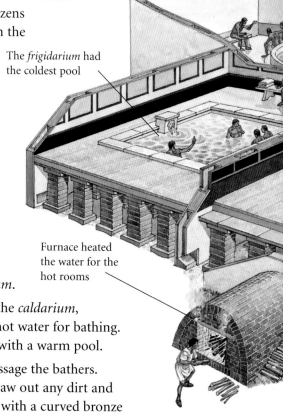

The *frigidarium* had the coldest pool

Furnace heated the water for the hot rooms

156

The *tepidarium* had a tepid, or cool, pool

◄ *A small public bath in a provincial town provides a hot bath, warm bath and cold plunge pool for the use of male citizens.*

The *caldarium* was the hottest room

● **The heat** for the hot rooms came from large furnaces located beside the baths. Hot air was piped under the floors and up cavities in the walls. Water was heated by the furnace in large copper pots.

● **Roman baths** were more than just places to get clean. There were also libraries, lounges, gardens and snack bars. Many men used the gardens and lounges as places to meet business contacts and discuss deals.

● **Women** went to the baths too but on different days to men.

● **Baths were often decorated** with marble panels and beautiful sculptures. The great baths built by the emperor Caracalla in AD 217, stood on the Celian Hill and remained in use until the aqueduct broke in AD 549. Today it is used as a venue for opera.

Roman roads

- **The most famous** of the Roman structures are the roads. Thousands of kilometres of road ran across the entire empire.

- **The construction** of Roman roads varied considerably depending on where they were, what materials could be found easily to hand and what its use would be.

- **In towns and cities**, roads were made of stone slabs laid over layers of sand that were packed down hard before the stones were put down. On either side of the road was an underground drain to carry away rainwater and dirt.

- **There was usually** a raised pavement on either side of city roads for pedestrians. Stepping stones allowed people to cross the road without treading in the horse dung and other mess that accumulated in the roadway.

- **In open country**, roads were surveyed by men who were trained to find the best route from one town to the next. Slaves were brought in to do the heavy labour. Army roads were built by soldiers.

- **Army roads** ran in long straight lines. This is because soldiers found it easier to march in a straight line, even up a steep hill, rather than to march along more level, windy roads.

▲ *Milestones were erected on roadsides to show distances between towns. Many showed which emperor was ruling at the time. This milestone bears the name Victorinus, who came to power in AD 269.*

▲ *The large flagstones that surface this Roman road were used only in towns or for heavily used stretches of road. Most roads were surfaced with gravel.*

- **Roads for civilian use** were not so straight. They were used by merchants and farmers with pack animals, or carts pulled by oxen or horses. Animals pulling heavy loads prefer to move on level roads, even if they are longer.

- **Roads** that were expected to take a lot of traffic were started by digging a trench about 12 m wide and setting large kerbstones along its sides. The trench was then filled with sand and gravel, which was packed down hard.

- **If the road** was close to a city or was to be used by important people, the upper surface was covered by slabs of stone that were curved to throw rainwater off to the sides.

- **Roads in rural areas** were rarely well-built. For most of their length they were dirt paths. In damp areas the road surface might be improved to stop it becoming muddy, while river crossings were improved with bridges or fords.

Bridges and arches

- **The Romans knew** that crossing rivers was often the most difficult part of a journey by road. People might get wet or lose possessions when crossing, and if the river was particularly high, there might be a long delay.

- **Fords** could be built up where the river was wide and shallow. Large quantities of stone and rock would be dumped into the river to form a firm foundation. On top of this was laid a flagstone surface, like an underwater road.

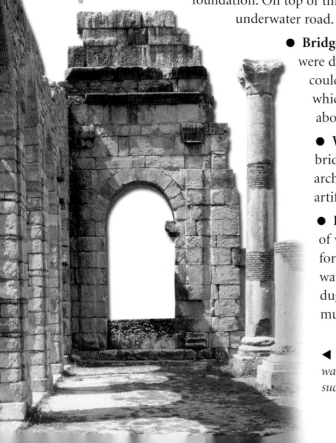

- **Bridges** were more effective where rivers were deeper or narrower. A narrow stream could be crossed by a single stone arch, which supported a humped road surface above.

- **Wider rivers** had to be crossed by bridges with more than one arch. Each arch was supported midstream by an artificial tower built up from the riverbed.

- **First**, the engineers hammered a circle of wooden stakes into the riverbed to form a watertight compartment. The water was pumped out and workmen dug out the riverbed to remove loose mud and reveal a firm surface.

◀ *The Roman arch enabled the weight of a wall to be spread evenly across an opening, such as a doorway or window.*

- **A stone tower** called a pier, was then built up to stand about 3 m above the river surface. The tower was usually wider and stronger at, and below, the water surface so that it could withstand floods.

- **On important roads** the bridge was completed by building a stone arch between each pier. On less important roads, wooden beams connected the piers. The road surface was then built on top.

▲ *The Ponte St Angelo, over the river Tiber in Rome, is carried on a succession of rounded arches.*

- **The Romans sometimes** built large arches over roads. These had no practical purpose, but were ornamental structures built to mark boundaries or commemorate famous events.

- **At Richborough** in Kent, there was a vast arch over the road that led up from the docks to the fort. This was the main military port for Britain. All soldiers entering or leaving Britain had to march through this arch.

- **In Rome**, a series of triumphal arches were built over the sacred road. These stone arches were decorated with carvings of battles and campaigns won by the general who was being honoured in the triumph.

161

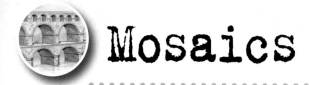

Mosaics

▼ *A mosaic of a dolphin made up of hundreds of pieces of coloured stone.*

- **One artform** that was perfected by the Romans was the mosaic. Several other ancient cultures made mosaics, but it was the Romans that used them most often and developed new an exciting styles.

- **A mosaic is a picture** made up of large numbers of small coloured stones, pieces of pottery or fragments of glass. Mosaics were often placed on floors as they are decorative and very hard wearing, but they may also be used on walls and ceilings.

- **Before creating a mosaic** the artist first draws a design that will fit the space of the right shape and size. He then collects enough pieces of stone, pottery or glass of the right size and colour for the design.

- **The floor is divided** into a number of smaller sections according to the artist's design. A section of floor is then covered with a smooth layer of wet plaster. The *tesserae*, as the small pieces of stone are known, are pushed into the plaster and rolled level.

- **Work on a mosaic** must be completed quickly before the plaster dries and hardens. Once the plaster has set, the design cannot be altered. Many mosaics have small errors in them that were not noticed until it was too late.

- **Especially complex** sections of design might be prefabricated. They were glued face down onto a roll of cloth using water-soluble glue. The cloth was then unrolled over the wet plaster. When the plaster had set, the cloth was soaked in water to loosen the glue, and then removed.

162

> **...FASCINATING FACT...**
> One house at Pompeii, south of Rome, had a mosaic in the doorway
> that was a picture of a dog with the words *cave canum* or 'beware of
> the dog' written beside it.

- **Master craftsmen** were hired to produce central panels showing animals,
  gods or men. Less skilled workers completed areas of plain colour,
  or geometric patterns around the edges.

- **Prestigious buildings** in Rome and other cities had mosaics made from
  chips of marble stone. These were the most durable and expensive types
  of mosaic.

- **Even houses** belonging to poor families would have a mosaic floor in rooms
  where visitors might enter in order to make a good impression.

▼ *An elaborate mosaic showing gods and goddesses in a ruined house. Mosaics such
as this were extremely expensive and could be afforded by only the richest families.*

Paintings

◀ *A Roman painting shows a lady being attended by a slave. Domestic scenes like this were favourite subjects.*

- **Painting** was an important form of art to the Romans. They painted pictures on walls, wooden panels and stone. Very few Roman paintings have survived.

- **Portraits of family** and friends were popular. These were usually painted onto wooden panels. They could be carried on journeys by soldiers or government officials.

- **Graves** were sometimes decorated with a portrait of the deceased person. While rich people would put up a stone carving, poorer people erected a wooden tablet with a portrait on.

- **In Egypt**, Roman families adopted the local custom of mummifying their bodies after death. A wooden portrait was then placed over the head.

- **Some paintings** became very famous. A picture of the Greek general Alexander the Great winning a battle has been copied many times and was made into a mosaic at least once.

▲ *A frieze of cherubs decorates a wall in a house at Pompeii.*
Details such as this were used in wall paintings to add interest.

- **The artist Veturius** became famous for painting designs on shields. It is thought he produced designs that were used by senior officers on parade. The designs may have included images of the gods.

- **Most wealthy Romans** had pictures painted on the walls of their houses. These paintings were called murals. The paint was applied while the wall plaster was still wet and this made them very durable.

- **The cheapest type** of mural was a design that made the walls look as if they were faced with marble or some other type of stone.

- **More elaborate murals** included paintings of statues, arches and doorways to make the house seem larger than it was. Some added windows with views across imaginary landscapes, or into gardens that did not really exist.

- **Some murals** have survived. Later building work buried some of Emperor Nero's palace, but the murals of statues and windows have survived.

Poems and histories

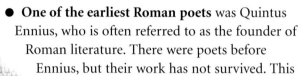

- **One of the earliest Roman poets** was Quintus Ennius, who is often referred to as the founder of Roman literature. There were poets before Ennius, but their work has not survived. This early work seems to have been dominated by short poems composed to honour a famous man, or an event.

- **Ennius began** by writing similar poems to those of earlier writers. Around 200 BC, he adopted Greek styles of rhythm and rhyme to Latin. Later poets copied him, and he became known as 'the father of Roman poetry'

▲ *The Roman writer Virgil wrote several books of poems as well as a history of Rome.*

- **In 180 BC**, Ennius began composing a poetic history of Rome that ran for 20,000 lines and took him over 15 years to complete. Only 550 lines have survived.

- **Titus Lucretius Carus**, known as Lucretrius, was a nobleman who began writing poetry about 75 BC. He compiled allusions to the gods and myths into works about nature and famous events.

- **The rich young politician**, Gaius Valerius Catullus (84–54 BC) , turned to writing poetry after an unhappy love affair. The works of Catullus are lyrical and have a steady rhythm. He wrote about everyday events, such as when the man next to him at dinner stole his napkin.

- **Quintus Horatius Flaccus** (65–27 BC), known as Horace, was the favourite poet of Emperor Augustus. Horace included lots of jokes and humour in his work – which was mostly in the form of short poems about life in Rome.

- **Publius Ovidius Naso** (AD 43–17), better known as Ovid, wrote beautiful love poems as well as more earthy works that poked fun at famous men and government officials. Because of this, he was exiled to a Greek city on the Black Sea by Augustus.

- **Sallust**, Gaius Sallustius Crispus (86–35 BC), was a politician who retired after the murder of Julius Caesar. He wrote histories of the civil wars and the careers of Marius and Sulla. He established a style of historic writing followed by all later historians.

- **Titus Livius**, better known as Livy, lived during the rule of Augustus. He wrote a history of Rome in 142 books, of which 35 survive. The Romans thought that he had produced the finest history of Rome ever written. Later historians concentrated on producing accounts of their own times.

...FASCINATING FACT...

The most famous work by Lucretius is *De Rerum Natura*, a poem running to six books in length. It shows a passionate concern for nature and all living things and includes vivid descriptions of forest fires, earthquakes and other natural events.

Oratory

- **Oratory**, the art of public speaking, was highly regarded in ancient Rome. It was taught to boys in secondary schools. Some scholars thought that oratory was the most important of all the arts.

- **Most Roman citizens** would be expected to speak in public at some stage of their lives. They would give their opinions during meetings of the *comitia*, speak out at meetings of local government and take part in court cases.

- **Even when a citizen** hired a lawyer for a court case, he was still expected to make a speech putting forward his point of view. Being able to speak with skill and confidence was vital.

- **Oratory** was a wide-ranging subject. The basics include the ability to speak clearly and loudly so that an entire audience could hear what was being said. A speaker had to be able to make points powerfully, be able to debate effectively and have a good knowledge of politics and philosophy.

- **Vocabulary** was a prized skill. This did not men knowing lots of different words, but knowing the precise meanings of words, and how to vary the intensity of meaning by putting different words together in a sentence.

- **History** was also included in the subject of oratory. It was thought to be useful to compare the subject of the speech with the actions of famous men from Rome's past.

> **...FASCINATING FACT...**
> Cicero rose to be consul in 62 BC, and made some of his most famous speeches in defence of the republican constitution in the face of attack by Julius Caesar. Cicero was executed in 43 BC after trying to oust Mark Antony from power.

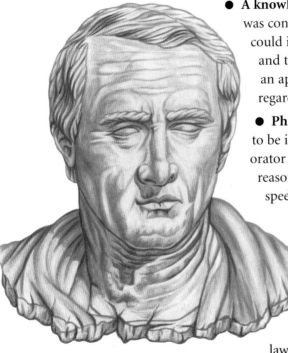

▲ *Cicero was a famous orator who was famous as the best speech-writer in Rome during the time of Julius Caesar.*

● **A knowledge of the gods** and religion was considered vital. An orator who could include references to the gods and their actions in his speech in an appropriate way was highly regarded.

● **Philosophy** was also considered to be important as it allowed an orator to produce underlying reasons why the subject of his speech was important, to persuade people to agree with him.

● **The Romans believed** that their greatest orator was Marcus Tullius Cicero (106–43 BC), a politician and lawyer who lived during the time of the civil wars. Many of Cicero's speeches were written down and used in schools.

On the stage

- **The Romans enjoyed** going to the theatre, which was enormously popular for many years. The first theatres were built around the year 200 BC, when the idea of staging plays was brought to Italy by the Greeks.

- **Roman theatres** were built in the open air and plays were performed during daylight. The theatres had a semi-circular stage with banks of seats rising up to enclose the rounded front edge of the stage.

- **Behind the stage** was a wooden or stone façade, built to resemble a town house. Many plays were written with characters going in and out of doors, or appearing on balconies to make the most of this backdrop.

- **When a different backdrop** was needed a painted curtain was hung up from the balconies of the house.

- **Actors dressed up** to appear like their characters. They also wore masks to help the audience recognize them whenever they appeared on stage.

- **One popular form** of comedy play was based around the legends of the gods. The plays showed deities and humans getting involved in ridiculous situations that were loosely based on well-known myths.

- **The very first plays** staged in Rome took place in 240 BC. They were Greek plays translated into Latin by a Greek playwright named Livius Andronicus.

◀ *Actors on stage wore masks to show which characters they were playing.*

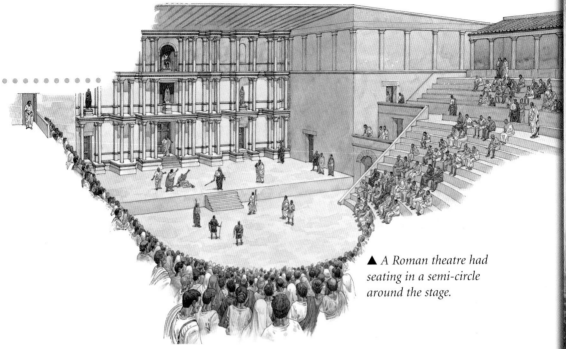

▲ *A Roman theatre had seating in a semi-circle around the stage.*

- **The first** popular plays in Rome were by Titus Maccius Plautus (*c* 250–184 BC). Plautus translated Greek plays, then added new jokes and references to Roman figures. These comedies included slapstick, puns and crude jokes.

- **The works of Terence**, Publius Terentius Afer (*c* 193 or 183–159 BC), are more sophisticated and cultured. Later Roman playwrights tended to write broad comedies like Plautus, or artistic works like Terence.

. . . FASCINATING FACT . . .
Most plays featured a limited number of characters. Among the most popular were the cunning slave, the strict father, the drunken son, the foolish wife, the angry neighbour, the dishonest cousin and the lovesick daughter.

Music and dance

- **The Romans used music** in a variety of ways to to provide fun and entertainment in their daily lives. Unfortunately, no Roman music has survived as they did not have a system for writing down tunes.

- **The Romans used wind instruments**, such as trumpets, flutes and a trumpet rather like a modern tuba. One very popular instrument was a twin set of pipes that were blown together, and played with one in each hand.

- **Two of the percussion instruments** that were widely used were the tambourine and cymbals. The clapping of hands was also used to give rhythm to music.

- **The most popular** stringed instrument was the lyre. This consisted of a series of strings stretched over a wooden frame and attached to a wooden box that increased the volume. It worked rather like a modern harp.

- **The loudest instrument** was the water organ. This complicated instrument was powered by air that was pumped into a metal pot held upside down in a tank of water. The air was kept pressurised, then blown out through pipes when buttons were pressed.

- **The daughters** of Roman citizens were expected to be able to play music to entertain their families at home.

- **Bands of professional** musicians were often hired to play music at dinners or other social events. Sometimes dancers were hired as well.

- **Music was often played** at the theatre. This helped to set the mood for the play. Serious music was played at emotional moments, and more fun music during comedies. Cymbals were clashed together when actors fell over.

- **Until about** AD **50**, no women were allowed on stage. Then some female musicians began to play at theatres and before long, actresses were also appearing.

- **Gladiatorial shows** were usually accompanied by bands of musicians. The music was played while the gladiators prepared to fight, while bodies were removed and while scenery or wild animals were being put in position.

◄ *Music was a favourite Roman art. Troupes of entertainers would be hired for special events.*

Statues and sculptures

▲ *Marble was used by most Roman sculptors as it can be carved in tiny detail.*

- **Until about 250 BC**, the Romans did not produce much sculpture. There were some wooden carvings in the temples, but none have survived. It was only when Greek-style architecture became fashionable that sculpture became common.

- **At first**, wealthy Romans bought statues and reliefs from Greece. Then, around 170 BC, they began commissioning new works. At first, these were copies of famous statues, but later, entirely new works began to be produced.

- **The most important** Roman invention in sculpture was the portrait bust. This was a statue of a person from the shoulders up that attempted to reproduce the features and appearance of the person.

- **From about 100 BC**, the Romans produced large numbers of portrait busts. Most were of famous men, but there were also busts of ordinary people.

- **Relief carvings** were produced to commemorate a specific event. A famous early example is the *Ara Pacis*, produced in 13 BC to celebrate a religious sacrifice held by Augustus to commemorate the end of the civil wars.

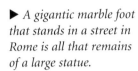

▶ *A gigantic marble foot that stands in a street in Rome is all that remains of a large statue.*

- **Commemorative** reliefs often featured on triumphal arches. By AD 50, copies were sent to province cities so that people living there could see them.

- **After the death** of Augustus, the emperors commissioned large numbers of statues of themselves to impress the public. Most show the emperor in formal dress and pouring a drink as an offering to the gods.

- **Trajan's column** is a 40-m-tall marble column in Rome that has a continuous frieze spiralling up it, showing scenes from Trajan's conquest of Dacia (modern-day Romania) in AD 106. The carvings reproduce military equipment in highly realistic detail.

- **A new style** of sculpture became common after about AD 175. This favoured movement and emotion rather than realism. Figures are shown in less detail, but they are running, jumping and walking with more vigour.

- **Nearly all Roman** sculpture that has survived is in stone. However, the Romans produced large numbers of bronze statues and sculptures as well. Most were melted down after the fall of the empire.

175

The Capitoline Triad

- **The three greatest gods** of ancient Rome were Jupiter, Juno and Minerva. They were honoured by a temple on top of the Capitoline Hill, and are known as the Capitoline Triad.

- **Jupiter** was the chief god of Rome. In his earliest appearances, Jupiter controlled all weather. He had a thunderbolt that he threw down to Earth to destroy anybody who offended the gods.

- **Jupiter symbolized** the virtues of justice and honour and kept promises. He was invoked when treaties were made, or war declared. He was sometimes called Jupiter Optimus Maximus, meaning 'the greatest and best' of the gods.

- **Juno** was the wife of Jupiter. She presided over family life and the private aspects of the Romans. Juno was invoked at weddings, births and around the time when children became adults.

▶ *Jupiter was the most important of the Roman gods. This is a copy of the statue of him that stood on the Capitoline Hill.*

- **Juno gave advice** to the Romans. In 390 BC, her sacred geese began to cackle when the Gauls tried to attack the Capitoline Hill. Consuls and emperors would pray to her when they needed advice about affairs of state.

- **Minerva** was originally an Etruscan goddess. Her worship was brought to Rome by King Tarquin Priscus. She was considered to be the goddess of wisdom and skill.

- **The first great temple** on the Capitoline Hill was built by Tarquin Priscus to honour the native Roman deities, Jupiter and Juno, as well as his new goddess, Minerva. The building was Greek in style, but was accidentally burnt down in 83 BC.

- **A new temple** to the Capitoline Triad was built. This temple covered two hectares of ground and was built on a rectangular platform of cut stones. A flight of 100 marble steps linked the temple to the Forum.

- **The temple** had three rows of columns across its front and two rows down either side. The floor was covered with sheets of bronze and the roof was covered with gold. The interior was decorated with numerous sculptures and trophies.

...FASCINATING FACT...
The worship of Minerva was strongest among workers such as potters, blacksmiths or musicians. She was also worshipped by warriors who wanted to gain greater skill in using weapons.

Gods of Rome

- **The Romans believed** in many gods and goddesses. Some of these were worshipped throughout the ancient world, others were only worshipped in Rome.

- **Janus** was a god found only in Rome. He had two faces, one at the front of his head, the other at the back so that he could look in opposite directions at the same time. He was the god of gates and doorways.

- **People prayed** to Janus when they passed through the gates of Rome on a journey. He became linked to the start of any journey or venture. The first month of the year was sacred to Janus and is still called January.

- **The temple of Janus** stood in the Forum over a natural spring of warm water. The main gates of the temple were kept shut during times of peace, but open in times of war.

- **Mars** was the father of Romulus and Remus. He had power over livestock, and each spring a bull, a ram and a boar were sacrificed to him.

◀ *The god Vulcan at work in his forge. He was believed to make weapons and tools for the gods.*

- **Mars is better known** as the god of war. Before a general left Rome to lead an army he went to the Temple of Mars to make a sacrifice, and pray to be given the power to instil terror in the enemy.

- **Inside the Temple of Mars** was an ancient shield that was said to have been left there by Mars himself. It was believed that as long as the shield was kept inside the temple, Rome would not be captured by an enemy.

- **Vulcan** was the god of fire. He was especially revered by smiths who needed a hot forge to work with, and by the disabled, as the god walked with a limp. An altar sacred to Vulcan stood in the Forum.

- **Egeria** was a goddess linked to springs and fresh water. She was the favourite goddess of King Numa. She was thought to be able to foretell the fate of newborn babies.

> ...FASCINATING FACT...
> The goddess Roma was the personification of the city of Rome.
> She was usually shown sitting on a rock, holding a spear and
> wearing a helmet on her head.

Gods of the city

- **People who lived in Rome** and other towns and cities throughout the empire, had their own gods and goddesses. Some were of Roman origin, others were borrowed from other cultures.

- **Tiberinus** was the god of the river Tiber. He was usually shown as a middle-aged man with a beard. Each year, on the 15 May, the Vestal Virgins carried 24 straw dolls to the Tiber and threw them in as a sacrifice to Tiberinus.

▼ *The portico of the Pantheon, a temple in Rome that was later converted to a church.*

- **Terminus was symbolized** by a block of stone set in the path that led up to the Temple of Jupiter from the Forum. He was god of property boundaries and his name was invoked during the purchase of land or houses.

- **Fides** was god of promises. People wishing to honour a promise would use his name. More serious was an oath sworn by the god Semo Sancus. He was thought to take revenge on people who broke a promise made in his name.

- **Fidius** was god of hospitality. He supervised meals and the guests who ate them. An insult given to a guest was considered an insult to Fidius.

- **Laverna** was goddess of thieves. She ensured that a burglar did not wake the people in the house that he had broken into, or could help a thief to escape from pursuit.

- **Victoria** was goddess of victory in battle. Once a battle had been won, she was replaced by Vitellia, goddess of military celebrations.

- **Concordia** was goddess of agreement and harmony in civil government. Officials worshipped her to ensure their decisions were popular.

- **Angerona** is a mysterious goddess. She is shown holding a finger up to her lips. She may have been the goddess of secrets whose name was invoked by those who did not want information to become public.

- **Pax** was the goddess of peace.

The Vestal Virgins

- **Vesta** was considered to be the most beautiful of all the goddesses of Rome. She was so lovely that when she came to the mortal world, she had to wear a veil to stop humans being blinded by her beauty. Statues of her always show a veiled woman.

- **Vesta was the goddess of the hearth**, and of fires used in homes for domestic purposes. Whenever a stove or grill was used for the first time, a portion of the meal had to be thrown into the flames as an offering to Vesta.

- **The temple of Vesta** was a round building that stood in the Forum. Only women were allowed to enter, and for most of the year the temple was closed to all except the six priestesses who were known as the Vestal Virgins.

- **Every five years**, a new Vestal Virgin was chosen at the age of six, by the *Pontifex Maximus*. He then shaved her head to symbolize her new birth as a priestess. The girl had to be free of any handicap or scar.

- **For the first ten years** of their service, the virgins were taught the secret rites of Vesta. For the next ten years, they carried out the rituals. For the third ten years, they taught new priestesses their tasks.

- **At the age of 36**, a Vestal Virgin was given the choice to leave the worship of Vesta to marry a Roman citizen, or to stay in the temple for the rest of her life.

- **The secret rituals** are long forgotten, but the public rituals involved keeping the sacred fire burning on the hearth of the temple and each day collecting a pot of water to put beside the fire.

- **The Vestal Virgins** were the only female priests in Rome. They were given a guard carrying an axe, and he escorted them whenever they went outside the temple of Vesta. Everyone had to step out of their way or risk being whipped in the Forum.

◀ *The priestesses of the goddess Vesta, who were traditionally known as the Vestal Virgins, leave their temple in procession. The chief festival of Vesta began on 7 June, when people came to offer food to the goddess.*

● **Whenever a festival** was held the best seats were reserved for the Vestal Virgins. A chariot was maintained at public expense for their sole use.

● **One power** of a Vestal Virgin was the ability to pardon any criminal of any crime, but only if she met him as he was led from his trial to his punishment.

183

Gods of the country

- **People who lived in rural areas** had their own gods. Most of these were connected to agriculture in some way, but some were deities of the wild and untamed lands that had not yet been been farmed.

- **Faunus** was the most important Roman agricultural god. He ensured that crops grew and ripened, and that animals produced plenty of young. He had a temple on the slopes of the Palatine Hill.

- **Consus** was the god of granaries (harvested or stored crops). He had no temple, only an altar that stood on the slopes of the Palatine Hill overlooking the Circus Maximus. For most of the year the altar was buried underground, but the earth was stripped off in December while crops were sown.

- **Pales** was a goddess who was thought to live beneath the Palatine Hill, to which she gave her name. She looked after the welfare of flocks of sheep and goats that roamed the hills and wilder areas of countryside.

- **Liber, and his wife Libera**, were the gods of the soil in farmland. At first, they were honoured by all farmers, but after about 100 BC, they became increasingly linked to the vine and so to winemaking.

- **Silvanus** was the god of forests and woodlands. He looked after the trees and was worshipped by the men who worked in forests, whether they were growing the trees or cutting timber.

- **Flora** was the goddess of flowers and of the spring. She had a temple on the Quirinal Hill that was guarded by a family called the Hirpini, who also supplied priests to the temple.

- **Vertumnus** was the god of fruit trees. He was deeply in love with Pomona, the goddess of apples, who lived in a sacred grove of apple trees a few kilometres west of Rome.

- **Ceres** was the goddess of growing corn and other grain crops. She had a small temple in Rome that was served by a single priest, who had to be a freed slave.

- **Venus** was a goddess who symbolized fertility among domestic animals, such as cattle and sheep. She was later linked to the Greek goddess, Aphrodite.

▲ *The goddess Venus was thought to have been born from the sea, and to have first reached dry land on the island of Cyprus riding on a giant shell.*

The lesser gods

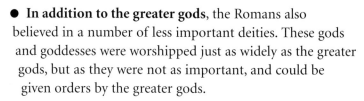

● **In addition to the greater gods,** the Romans also believed in a number of less important deities. These gods and goddesses were worshipped just as widely as the greater gods, but as they were not as important, and could be given orders by the greater gods.

● **Fortuna** was a goddess who took particular interest in the affairs of humans. If she liked a person she would give them good luck, but if she disliked someone they would suffer only bad luck.

● **The main temple** to Fortuna was at the town of Praeneste in central Italy, where the chief priest was able to tell visitors whether or not Fortuna liked them at that moment.

● **A small, solid gold statue** of Fortuna was kept by Augustus, in his bedroom. He left it to Tiberius and it became part of the inheritance of the emperors. As late as the reign of Marcus Aurelius, it remained in the imperial bedroom.

● **The god Saturnus** lived underground where he supervised the fertility of the soil. The festival Saturnalia was held in December in his honour. It involved feasting and gift-giving.

◄ *A snake twined around a stick was the symbol of Aesclepius, god of healing.*

186

- **Mercurius** was the god of merchants. He had a temple on the Aventine Hill where sacred cockerels were kept in his honour. Mercury's daughter, Pecunia, was the patron goddess of profits.

- **Because merchants** often carried messages when they travelled on business, Mercury later became the god of messengers. He was thought to be the messenger of the gods and was shown with a winged helmet and sandals.

- **Aeneas** was a deity whose origins lie in Asia. He was said to be a great warrior who fought against the Greeks during the siege of Troy. When Troy fell in about 1300 BC, Aeneas led the surviving Trojans on a long journey that ended in Italy.

- **As the ancestor** of the Romans, Aeneas was much respected, but he was not thought to have any particular powers.

- **Spes** was the god of hope. In the earliest times, the Romans prayed to Spes when they were ill and they bathed in pools of water that were sacred to him. Romans later preferred the Greek god of healing, Aesclepius.

◀ *The Fates. They spun thread and wove cloth that symbolized the lives of humans.*

The Underworld

- **The Romans believed** that a dead person's soul was grabbed by two spirits, one pulling from the front, the other pushing from behind. The spirits led the soul deep underground to the land of Hades to meet the god Dis, who would decide its fate.

- **Dis** met the soul and read out from a scroll the deeds that the person had performed while alive. If there were more deeds that pleased the gods than displeased them, the soul was allowed to enter Hades.

- **If a person had committed** more acts that displeased the gods, the soul would be handed over to the goddess Tuchulcha, and her husband, Charon. Tuchulcha had eyes of fire, pointed ears and snakes wrapped around her body.

- **Februus** was the god who caused death. He walked across the Earth searching for those whose lives were coming to an end. The second month of the year was sacred to him, and is still called February.

- **Lara** was a terrifying goddess who hated naughty children. She stalked around searching for the naughtiest children to drag them off to Hades. She could not talk, and moved silently.

- **The Manes**, or the good ones, were the servants of Dis who were thought to visit the Earth for several days each year. During this time, all temples were closed and business deals could not be concluded.

- **When a person died**, the body was dressed in the finest clothes available and laid out in their house overnight. Friends and relatives gathered to pay their respects.

- **A procession** carried the body from the house, out of the city gates to a special place set aside for funerals. People who had known the deceased made speeches to honour his or her memory.

- **The body was burned** on a fire. The ashes were gathered up after the fire had died down and placed in a special jar called an urn.

- **Rich families** had large tombs placed alongside a main road leading out of the city into which urns were placed. Poorer families put their urns into underground communal tombs called *catacombs*, or simply buried them in the ground.

▼ *When people died, their souls were thought to be carried by the ferryman, Charon, across a sacred river to the Underworld.*

Family gods

- **Each Roman family** had a number of deities that were sacred to them, and to nobody else. It was believed that these gods took care of the members of the family.

- **The most important** family gods were the *lares*. The *lares* may have been a deified ancestor of the family. Each family had a small wooden statue of their *lares* placed in a small shrine somewhere in the house.

- **Whenever a person** joined or left the family, a sacrifice had to be made to the *lares*. If a woman joined the family by marriage, or a man was adopted, incense and wine had to be offered to the *lares*.

- **After a funeral**, another sacrifice had to be made to the *lares*. Rich families offered two sheep, but poorer families probably offered just some bones and fat from a sheep.

- **Viriplaca** was a goddess who had the task of soothing quarrels within a family. A small statuette of Viriplaca might be placed alongside that of the *lares* if the head of the family wanted to see a dispute ended.

◀ *A gladiator prays to a shrine sacred to the god Mars. Small places of worship were commonplace.*

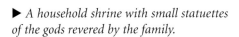

▶ *A household shrine with small statuettes of the gods revered by the family.*

- **Each household** had two *Penates*. Small figures of these two gods were placed near the entrance to a house. Their main task was to care for the food of the family, making sure that stored food did not go bad.

- **When a meal was served**, a small sample of the food was put before the statuettes of the *Penates*. This was so that the gods could bless the food and make sure that it was nutritious.

- **When a baby was born**, the gods were believed to send a 'genius' to care for it. This genius stayed with the person all through life, returning to the gods only when that person died.

- **The genius** was thought to summon other spirits to help it. Vaticanus helped the baby to speak, Educa taught it to eat and Ossipago made sure that its bones grew properly. Adeona helped the child learn to walk while Sentinus helped it become intelligent.

- **Each person** was expected to honour his or her genius on their birthday. A small amount of wine, or some flowers were offered at a shrine to the genius. There was a short ritual dance that was supposed to be performed.

Gods from Greece

- **Before about 300 BC**, the Romans did not have a clear idea of where the world had come from nor how the gods had come into existence. They believed that the gods and humans had always existed and always would.

- **After that date**, the Romans began to come into contact with peoples with more advanced religious ideas. The Etruscans thought that everything had been created by a god named Summanus, who even created the other gods.

- **More influential** were the ideas from Greece. The Greeks believed in a complex story in which the universe emerged from dark chaos through the intervention of powerful forces. The Greek gods played an important role in this creation story.

  - **The Romans thought** that the Greek version of creation was probably true. They adopted the story of dark chaos and generations of gods, and adapted the story to suit Roman views and ideas.

  - **The Romans also adopted** some of the Greek gods. The most popular Greek gods in Rome were those that looked after an activity or subject that was not already cared for by the native Roman and Italian gods.

    - **The most popular** Greek god in Rome was Apollo. This god of music, light and healing could give prophecies to humans, or send sudden death. Demeter, a goddess of growing crops, was also popular.

◀ *The god Apollo was usually shown as a handsome young man.*

▶ The water god Neptune was usually shown as an old man with a long beard and long hair.

- **The Romans also believed** that some of their own gods and Greek gods were the same divine beings, but just known by different names. They merged the powers and personalities of these pairs of gods.

- **The Roman goddess Venus** was concerned with fertility, as was the Greek goddess, Aphrodite. Aphrodite was also the goddess of love, so Venus became the Roman goddess of love.

- **The Roman god Neptune** was the god of water, with dozens of children and associates to look after individual seas, lakes or rivers. The Greek god Poseidon was god of the seas, but also had an important role in the Greek creation myth. Neptune became very like Poseidon, losing his powers over fresh water, but gaining a role in creation.

- **The Roman goddess Diana** and the Greek goddess Artemis were both woodland deities linked to hunting and the moon. Diana soon acquired all the stories that were told in Greece about Artemis.

Provincial deities

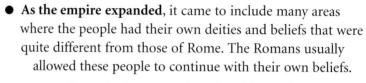

- **As the empire expanded**, it came to include many areas where the people had their own deities and beliefs that were quite different from those of Rome. The Romans usually allowed these people to continue with their own beliefs.

  - **Egypt had many** gods and goddesses that had been worshipped for over 3000 years. Ra, the sun god, was said to be the creator of heaven and earth.

  - **Osiris** was the Egyptian god of the dead. He was believed to have taught the Egyptians the skills of civilization and law and order before becoming ruler of the kingdom of the dead.

  - **Hathor**, daughter of Ra, was the goddess of joy and love, and the protector of women. Hathor was usually shown as a woman with a cow's head.

  - **The greatest god** of the Phoenicians, who lived in what is now Palestine, Israel and Lebanon, was El. It was El who caused rains to fall and rivers to flow, thus allowing crops to grow in this arid area.

  - **Adonis** was the most handsome of the Phoenician gods. He was a god of growing plants and spent half of the year on earth supervising crops and wild plants, and half of the year among the gods.

◀ *The goddess Brigantia from Britain was a powerful goddess of the Celts.*

- **The Celts** had a large number of deities, some of which the Romans thought were the same as their own gods, but with different names. Sulis, the water goddess of Britain, was identified with Minerva.

- **Epona** was the Celtic horse goddess. The white horse of Uffington, a chalk hill figure, was probably sacred to Epona. This goddess was widely worshipped by cavalry units in the Roman army.

- **Lug of the Long Arm** was a Celtic god of craftsmen, especially of carpenters and blacksmiths. In carvings, he is usually shown holding a spear, and some legends have him fighting as a warrior.

▶ *Ra, the Egyptian sun god. He was sometimes worshipped together with Re (also known as Ra) as Atum-Re.*

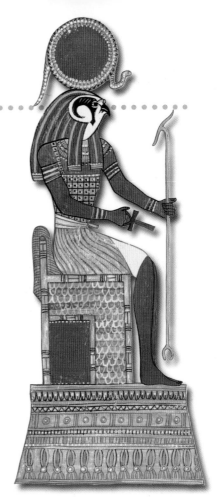

...FASCINATING FACT...
The Druids were the priests of the Celts. They organized rituals, and acted as judges. When the Druids organized a holy war against the Romans, the Romans reacted by ruthlessly killing them all. It was a rare example of religious intolerance.

Cult religions

- **The Romans came to adopt** many cult religions from the countries that they conquered, mostly from the eastern provinces. These cults were often looked upon with suspicion because the rituals took place in private.

- **The most widespread** cult was the worship of the Persian god Mithras. He was believed to have given fertility to the barren earth by killing a sacred bull and allowing the blood to flow over the world.

- **Mithraism** taught that each person had an immortal soul. After death, the powers of light and darkness compete to grab the soul for all eternity. Mithras could intervene in this struggle to help his worshippers go to the light.

- **The followers of Mithras** met in underground temples, usually dominated by a statue or carving of the god killing the sacred bull. There were seven ranks of worshipper, and the religion was particularly popular among Roman soldiers, who believed it gave life after death.

▲ *The Persian god Mithras is usually shown killing a bull.*

- **Dionysus** was a Greek nature god who was also linked to the production of wine. He was said to have married Ariadne, daughter of the king of Crete, and made her immortal so that their love would never die.

- **The the cult of Dionysus** involved rituals that included the drinking of large quantities of wine. Followers believed that if they proved worthy of the god's love he would immortalize them, and let them live with him after death.

- **Orpheus** was a semi-divine musician who supposedly charmed wild animals into obedience. The Orphics sang sacred songs as part of their rituals.

▲ *Temples to Mithras were usually built without windows to mimic the dark cave in which he killed the bull.*

- **The Orphics believed** the soul could be purified by not eating meat, living a simple life and avoiding sinful actions. A purified soul would live again as another human being and an impure soul would be destroyed.

- **The Egyptian goddess Isis** became the centre for a cult that revolved around the reading of sacred texts and poems. Isis was thought to be the mother of all the gods and to have absolute power over the Earth.

- **Cybele** was a mother goddess from what is now Turkey. Women who were initiated into her cult had to bathe in bull's blood. The women were then sacred to Cybele, and her husband, Attis.

197

Humans become gods

- **The division between** the human and the divine was not always clear. The Romans believed that the gods sometimes walked on Earth and interfered in the affairs of humans. Men who especially pleased the gods might be taken to live among them after death.

- **The Roman Senate** had the power to declare that a person had been so beloved of the gods that he had become one with them. A wooden statue of the person was carved, and burned on a large fire so that the flames would carry the soul of the dead up to heaven.

- **After his death**, Julius Caesar was deified by the Senate. This helped Augustus to gain the support of many people as he had the prestige of being the nephew of a god.

- **The people** of several eastern provinces were accustomed to worshipping their kings and rulers as if they were gods. Some of them wanted to worship Augustus as a god.

- **Augustus compromised** by allowing the eastern peoples to worship his genius. This allowed them to continue their usual customs without upsetting the Romans, who did not believe men could become gods before their death.

- **After his death**, Augustus was deified, as was Tiberius. The next emperor, Caligula, had his sister Drusilla deified after her death.

- **Caligula did not want** to wait until death to become a god. He ordered that the people in the east should worship him, not his genius. He announced that he was a god and built a temple to himself on the Palatine Hill.

- **Caligula began to dress** as the different gods, and even as goddesses. He would enter temples and talk to the statues of the deity as if holding a conversation with them. People began to think he had gone mad.

- **The next emperor**, Claudius, was more cautious. He ordered that he could be worshipped as a god in the provinces if the people liked, but he was not to be considered a god in Rome. Soon after his death he was deified by the Senate.

- **Later emperors** followed the policy of Claudius. When the emperor Vespasian was told that he was dying, he laughed and said, "Oh dear. It seems that I am about to become a god."

◄ *The Temple of Claudius was built at Colchester in the province of Britannia. Many emperors were declared to be gods after they died.*

199

Rituals and sacrifices

- **The Romans had many** religious festivals that took place throughout the year. Some of them involved everyone in Rome, and meant that businesses closed for the day. Others were observed only by priests or priestesses.

- **Most gods and goddesses** had a temple, or temples, dedicated to their worship. The temple usually stood on a raised platform, and contained a large public room in which stood a statue of the deity. There might also be other rooms for the use of the priests.

- **No services** or rituals took place inside the temple, which was considered to be the house of the god. People were free to enter the temple to pray or to hand over offerings to the priests.

- **The rituals** took place at an altar outside the the temple. The usual form of ritual was a sacrifice. Small amounts of wine or incense were offered daily.

- **More elaborate rituals** and sacrifices took place on festivals sacred to the god or goddess worshipped at the temple. Unlike the rituals of the cults, these rituals took place in public so that everyone could watch.

> ...FASCINATING FACT...
> Priests might attempt to predict the future by inspecting the livers of sacrificed animals. Some priests might try to help a person by inflicting a curse on an enemy or rival. Some curses were written on stone tablets that were then buried, or thrown into ponds or wells.

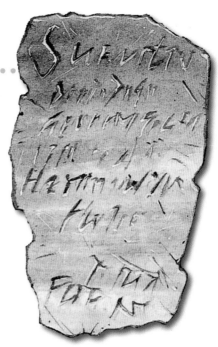

▶ *A curse written on a shard of stone would be buried close to a temple in the hope that the god would make the curse come true.*

- **On 23 July**, the Neptunalia took place in honour of Neptune, god of the sea. People gathered at the temple of Neptune to pray for rain to fall in the dry season. They built miniature huts out of twigs, perhaps as symbolic shelter from rain.

- **The oldest** of the festivals in Rome was the *Ludi Romani*, or 'Roman games'. These took place each summer in the Circus Maximus. The festival was sacred to Jupiter.

- **The *Ludi Romani*** began with a sacrifice in the Capitoline Temple. After this, there were athletic contests in the Circus Maximus. The festival ended with a series of chariot races.

- **The festival of *Ambarvalia*** was held on 29 May in honour of the god Mars, who was originally in charge of agriculture. As Mars evolved into God of War, many of his agricultural duties were assigned to the goddess Ceres. During the *Ambarvalia*, animals were slaughtered in the hope that crops would be purified and the harvest plentiful.

Festivals

- **The greatest** festival was *Saturnalia*, held in honour of the god, Saturn. It lasted seven days. *Saturnalia* began on 17 December, when the priests of Saturn entered the temple that stood at the foot of the Capitoline Hill.

- **At dawn,** the priests of Saturn untied ropes of wool that held Saturn inside his temple for most of the year. The god was then free to wander the Earth. Everyone washed themselves so that they were clean if they met the god.

- **While the priests** of Saturn carried out rituals inside their temple, all public buildings were closed and locked. Schools were closed down, no law cases could proceed and the Forum was closed to business.

- **When the rituals ended**, the feasting began. People wore simple tunics with no sign of their status in society. In particular, the toga that marked a man as a citizen of Rome was taken off.

- **The god Vulcan** was honoured in the festival of *Volcanalia*, which was held on 23 August, the hottest part of the year. Priests carried out rituals at the god's altar, then marched to the Tiber, where live fish were thrown onto a fire in the hope that Vulcan would spare citizens from heat of summer.

- *Lupercalia* was held on 15 February in honour of the god, Faunus. This was considered to be a very important festival and all the inhabitants of Rome were expected to be out on the streets to celebrate it.

> **...FASCINATING FACT...**
> Slaves were freed for *Saturnalia*. They could say or do what they liked, but had to return home at the end of the festival. *Saturnalia* lasted seven days, ending on 24 December.

▲ *A Triumph parade marches through Rome. Triumphs were held to welcome commanders back to Rome who had won a military victory.*

- **The festival began** when the priests of Faunus sacrificed goats on the altar outside the temple. The goat skins were then used to make cloaks for the priests and whips for them to carry. Two young men were smeared with goat's blood and had to laugh out loud.

- **The priests of Faunus** ran through the streets of Rome. They were naked except for the goat skins, and they used the whips to lash out at women they met. To be struck by the whips was considered to be good luck.

- **Triumphs** were military or political clebrations. A Triumph was held when a successful general and his army returned from a successful battle. The general rode in a chariot, leading his army to the Temple of Jupiter where sacrifices were made.

The rise of Christianity

- **In about the year** AD **40**, Christianity began to spread across the Roman Empire. The religion began with the life and teachings of a Jew named Jesus and, at first, spread among the Jewish communities.

- **Christianity** spread gradually outside the Jewish communities to other provinces of the Roman Empire. Christianity was, for many centuries, the faith of a minority of the population of the empire.

- **In about the year** AD **50**, a Christian leader named Peter came to Rome. He organized the small Christian community in Rome, and was later regarded as having been the first Bishop, or Pope, of Rome.

- **In** AD **64**, a large area of Rome burnt down. The emperor Nero blamed this on the Christians, which resulted in many Christians being executed.

- **Meanwhile**, a Christian leader named Paul was spreading the religion through the eastern part of the empire. By AD 100, small Christian communities existed in most provinces of the empire.

▲ *An early Christian prays in a secret, underground church. Some emperors persecuted the Christians.*

- **Christianity** had many followers by around AD 200. However, Christian communities were split by disputes about the nature of Jesus, mainly over the issue of whether he was human, divine or both.

- **By this date**, most Romans saw Christianity as a successful religion, and did not see it as a threat to their own gods. However, the Christians believed that all other gods were evil and that their worship should be stopped.

▲ *A mosaic showing the head of Christ. By the time this mosaic was made, about AD 350, many Romans were Christians.*

- **In AD 303**, Emperor Diocletian ordered a persecution of the Christians. All Christian books were destroyed, churches closed, and no Christians were allowed to hold government jobs. He thought Christian opposition to traditional gods opposed the rule of Rome.

- **Emperor Constantine** made Christianity legal again in AD 313, when he became a Christian himself. Constantine then confiscated the wealth of the pagan temples, some of which was used to build Christian churches.

- **In AD 360**, the pagan, Julian, became emperor. He did not persecute the Christians, but promoted his own religion. He failed. In AD 391, Emperor Theodosius I closed pagan temples and made pagan worship illegal.

The eternal city

- **The city of Rome** fell to the barbarian king, Alaric of the Visigoths, in the year AD 410. The news shocked people throughout the entire empire.

- **After the sacking** of Rome by the Goths in AD 410 and the Vandals in AD 455, urban life continued in the city. The population fell dramatically, but the people who remained were part of the empire.

- **The last emperor** in the west abdicated in AD 476. At first, few people noticed as the move was thought to be only temporary.

- **In the east**, an emperor continued to rule from Constantinople. The culture of the eastern empire changed, becoming more Greek than Roman. The eastern empire did not fall until 1453.

- **In the west**, a succession of barbarian kings ruled the areas that had formerly been the Roman Empire. They led a military elite, but most people were the descendents of the population of the Roman Empire.

◄ *Castel St Angelo was originally built as a tomb for Emperor Hadrian around* AD *135. During the Middle Ages it was converted into a fortress. It shows how modern Rome has adapted and used its ancient heritage.*

● **People in Spain**, Gaul (France), Italy and elsewhere continued to speak Latin. The languages of those countries today is based on Latin. They lived according to Roman laws, and the legal codes of those countries are derived from those of Rome.

● **In Britain**, the country was invaded by Germanic tribes. Roman law was forgotten, and Latin was replaced by English. Only in remote areas was Christianity retained.

● **The Christian church** preserved much of the Roman culture. Latin remained the language of the Church until the 20th century. Special robes worn by bishops and cardinals today, are based on those of ancient Rome.

● **The bishops of Rome**, the popes, were able to combine the authority handed down by Peter and the prestige of the city of Rome to become the most important bishops in Christendom.

● **There is a saying** in Rome, 'While the Colosseum stands, Rome will stand. When the Colosseum falls, Rome will fall.' The Colosseum is still standing.

207

Index

Index

Index

Index

Index

Acknowledgements

All artworks are from the Miles Kelly Artwork Bank

The publishers would like to thank the following picture sources whose photographs appear in this book:

Page 4 jundangoy/Fotolia.com
Page 9 The British Museum/HIP/Topfoto.co.uk
Page 12 2006 Alinari/Topfoto.co.uk
Page 14 The British Museum/HIP/Topfoto.co.uk
Page 19 Albo/Fotolia.com
Page 20 Art Media/HIP/Topfoto.co.uk
Page 26 Charles Walker/Topfoto.co.uk
Page 39 Roger-Viollet/Topfoto.co.uk
Page 49 Dana Russow/Fotolia.com
Page 82 Topham Picturepoint/Topfoto.co.uk
Page 112 javarman/Fotolia.com
Page 114 Stapleton Collection/Corbis
Page 121 Wai Heng Chow/Fotolia.com
Page 136 Andrea Seemann.Fotolia.com
Page 144 Stapleton Collection/Corbis
Page 161 NYPhotoboy/Fotolia.com
Page 178 Topfoto.co.uk
Page 182 Christie's Images/Corbis
Page 189 Charles Walker/Topfoto.co.uk
Page 197 Museum of London/HIP/Topfoto.co.uk
Page 206 tzam66/Fotolia.com

All other photographs from:

Castrol, CMCD, Corbis, Corel, digitalSTOCK, digitalvision
Flat Earth, Hemera, ILN, John Foxx, PhotoAlto, PhotoDisc
PhotoEssentials, PhotoPro, Stockbyte